ROOTS IN THE AIR

ALSO BY SHIRLEY KAUFMAN

The Floor Keeps Turning
Gold Country
Looking at Henry Moore's Elephant Skull Etchings in Jerusalem
    During the War
From One Life to Another
Claims
Rivers of Salt

TRANSLATIONS

A Canopy in the Desert, translated from the Hebrew of Abba
    Kovner
My Little Sister and Selected Poems, translated from the Hebrew
    of Abba Kovner
The Light of Lost Suns, translated from the Hebrew of Amir
    Gilboa
But What: Selected Poems of Judith Herzberg, translated from the
    Dutch with the poet

SHIRLEY KAUFMAN

ROOTS
IN THE AIR

NEW & SELECTED POEMS

COPPER CANYON PRESS

Publication of this book is supported by a grant from the National
Endowment for the Arts and a grant from the Lannan Foundation.
Additional support to Copper Canyon Press has been provided by the
Andrew W. Mellon Foundation, the Lila Wallace–Reader's Digest
Fund, and the Washington State Arts Commission. Copper Canyon
Press is in residence with Centrum at Fort Worden State Park.

Library of Congress Cataloging-in-Publication Data
Kaufman, Shirley
Roots in the air: new and selected poems / by Shirley Kaufman
p. cm.
ISBN 1-55659-055-5
1. Title.
PS3561.A862R66 1996
811'54 – DC 20   96-10009

COPPER CANYON PRESS
P.O. BOX 271, PORT TOWNSEND, WASHINGTON 98368

ACKNOWLEDGMENTS

The selected poems have been taken from *The Floor Keeps
Turning*, 1970, *Gold Country*, 1973, *From One Life to Another*,
1979, all published by the University of Pittsburgh Press; from
Claims, The Sheep Meadow Press, 1984; and from *Rivers of Salt*,
Copper Canyon Press, 1993. I am especially grateful to the
poet-editors of these books, Paul Zimmer, Stanley Moss, and
Sam Hamill, for their steadfast friendship and encouragement
over the years.

"Looking at Henry Moore's Elephant Skull Etchings in Jeru-
salem During the War" was first published as a book, with the
Moore etchings, by Unicorn Press, 1977; second edition, 1979.

Some of the new poems, often in earlier versions, have previ-
ously appeared in the following periodicals: *The American Poetry
Review*, *Arc*, *Ariel*, *Field*, *Nimrod*, *Poetry Ireland Review*, and *The
Tel Aviv Review*.

"Mortality" first appeared in *Switched-On Gutenberg*, an elec-
tronic poetry journal on Internet.

My gratitude to Lois Bar-Yaacov and Ruth Nevo in Jerusalem,
and the many friends everywhere who have helped me immea-
surably, shared my concerns, and continue to sustain me. And
most of all, to my husband, Bill Daleski, who has made this
book, and everything else, possible.

To my daughters
Sharon, Joan, Deborah

with love and admiration

Contents

I

from The Floor Keeps Turning
1970

But it was right that she
looked back. Not to be
curious, some lumpy
reaching of the mind
that turns all shapes to pillars.
But to be only who she was
apart from them, the place
exploding, and herself
defined. Seeing them melt
to slag heaps and the flames
slide into their mouths.
Testing her own lips then,
the coolness, till
she could taste the salt.

Natives of Chagos
strip the shell
from living turtles.

They buck through
the delicate coral,
where men ride them
down to tie them,
heaping their backs
with fire.
        Travelers
have seen the bony
back
     crack upward,
flames climbing
the curling shell.

Knives force it
from them. Living,
they go on living,
soft, gelatinous
bodies like sinking
rafts.
        They weep
in the water, bury
their sad eyes. Return
in a new shell
thin as an old man's
skin.
        Grieve more
than a hundred

years,

       die usually
from accidents.

1

My bones lengthen,
grow silently to their own causes.
Even my ankles are changing,
skin of my instep
stretches over the arch.
My arms are wrapped in thick fur;
carnivorous birds fly out of my wrists
when we begin to stroke the air.

2

Safer than rooms,
whatever hollow in the earth
I made, small-breasted as a child,
and knew by other faces
in the dark. Now graffiti
on the walls glitter
like an old family; those ancient
bulls keep watch.
Amber and ochre, color
of winter pears. They glow,
purely the cave's invention,
and we move in them reflected,
reach for unchanging signs
and give off light.

3

You bring me distance, warm
vineyards sloping to Lac Léman,

evenly terraced as your breathing evenly
without dreams. That castle in Lausanne.
The queen of Spain slept there, they said,
as if a throne climbed into bed
with castanets. Dark oak
and deeply carved. The skin of a queen
must be softer than tongues
when she leans against great pillows.
Rainwater, when you drown
your fingers in it. Deep.

4

"Je suis belle"…as a sleep of stone:
you seek that part of me
I would not lose,
just as those Rodin hands
in their tense bronze sob
in the flesh of her giving
and withholding. She bends
and folds over, exceeding herself.
And he lifts her, lifts her,
clutches her smoothness, thrusts
his chin into the moss of her neck.

5

The night is alive with shadows,
ships scraping up to the docks,
waves slapping around the wood,
bulkheads creaking, queens sailing
into a storm, cinders
of spray – such motion in the wind
that everything gives way – anchor

and line, shape of that wrinkled harbor,
and we rock, we rock,
we rock and we are visible
each to to the other as nothing
was ever visible before.

FOR REGGIE KRISS

Hills moved. I watched their shadows
riding by like names said
only once. The oaks turned round
and leaves ran past my head.

It was all reeling back where
the old disasters hung between
locked doors stitching the air,
unheard, as if they'd never been.

And the sun came falling through
the window of the train; it filled
my lap, slid down my arms into
the aisle, a blazing river spilled

inside. I found her in the shallow
light, wearing her skeleton
strapped smooth over her belly,
wallowing on her back, alone.

Some little Pequod spitting, mastheads
tufted with joints like unfleshed frogs,
lame as a butterfly spread
on a pin. And from the thrashing legs

hooks caught at nothing, casting
and casting in the air, her
bent and beaded feelers lashing
until the threads would have to tear.

Pharaohs watched her push her dung ball
on the sand the way the sun
rolled slowly over heaven, saw
how she hatched her children

out of that roundness, called her Life.
They made her image out of stone,
greener than stems, to celebrate
the ornamental lake a queen

had built, to mark a lion hunt
or even marriage. They sent
her gleaming in the tombs of all
the dead so they might rise again.

I didn't touch her; slipping a marker
from my book under her back,
I turned my wrist down gently, set her
right. A piece of the whole shook

world turned up. Alive! She was
amazed to flex herself, to feel
the sun along her side like juice,
to have her front legs wheel

her forward, arched in a priestly
benediction. Oh she was tight. She served
her concentrated self, and neatly.
Her eyes glittered out of her head.

Lightly she went and steady down
the aisle. Not any landscape she
remembered. Yet she was sure of home,
composed her dark wherever she might be

creeping. I waved her well. Saw
that she left no furrow in the floor.
But someone got up, swelling out
of his seat and raised his foot, before

my hand could drop, and put it down
and passed into the next car
and was gone. There was no sound
but the train's sound. Far

down the tracks, the sun rolled over.
I had to sit there after that
and look at California moving
backward, pressing my face flat

against the glass until it froze
to my skin. All afternoon
I looked out at the hills, those
trees with the light crawling down

their branches like white beetles
and the sky lurching among
the leaves, the shape of it tilting
at me crushed under the sun.

"IF I HAD FOUND IT, BELIEVE ME, I SHOULD HAVE MADE NO
FUSS AND STUFFED MYSELF LIKE YOU OR ANYONE ELSE."

Franz Kafka

1

It's no use trying to find again
what it was like.
And the spectacle of it. The breasts
begin to go, skin
loosens under the chin.
You watch
an aging courtesan undress.

2

Him waiting, waiting as if
you never loved by night.
Long welts
of daylight, another bed.
To let it happen
easy as Eden, no wringing
of the mind, wrestle of leaves
to squeeze through.
His solemn arms, his room
not dark enough, your having
to be the way you are.
You fasten like things on a pond
to their own reflection.
Till he discovers that
you cannot play.

Remember your swimming
when a wave fell in.
Too stunned to fight the undertow,
you gave yourself up
dreaming to the pull.
When you lie down once more
in dangerous places
taking the fruit between your teeth,
there is always the light
thatched over another
who breathes beside you, entire,
strange to your wanting
even the least of what he was.

4

When plastic chairs in the kitchen
begin to crack, or fabric
on the footstool wears
through to the stuffing,
or the sink falls slowly down
from the level of the Formica counter
because water got in
under the unseen wood and is secretly
chewing it all away;

when you look in the mirror
after everyone leaves in the morning,
and the only sound is the thin hum
of the furnace, and suddenly
it stops, and the house begins to tick,
and you see the small wrinkles

under your lashes smudged
with mascara you never get off,
and you make a terrible smile
watching them deepen and lengthen
like thin lines raked in the sand
of a perfect Japanese garden;

you feel everything
being eaten from its surface.
Soon there will be no covers
and what is under
will be exposed, wasted,
no longer able
to keep the flesh alive.

Mothers, Daughters

Through every night we hate,
preparing the next day's
war. She bangs the door.
Her face laps up my own
despair, the sour, brown eyes,
the heavy hair she won't
tie back. She's cruel,
as if my private meanness
found a way to punish us.

We gnaw at each other's
skulls. Give me what's mine.
I'd haul her back, choking
myself in her, herself
in me. There is a book
called Poisons on her shelf.
Her room stinks with incense,
animal turds, hamsters
she strokes like silk. They
exercise on the bathroom
floor, and two drop through
the furnace vent. The whole
house smells of the accident,
the hot skins, the small
flesh rotting. Six days
we turn the gas up then
to fry the dead. I'd fry
her head if I could until
she cried love, love me!

All she won't let me do.
Her stringy figure in
the windowed room shares
its thin bones with no one.
Only her shadow on the glass
waits like an older sister.
Now she stalks, leans forward,
concentrates merely on getting
from here to there. Her feet
are bare. I hear her breathe
where I can't get in. If I
break through to her, she will
drive nails into my tongue.

Eye

1

If she were Greek
she would have killed me,
axed the mother
out of the play
         the way
a daughter's fury works.

I lie in my bandage of dark,
smelling orange and cabbage,
hearing the sounds of their seeing
TV the dishes the faucet everything
going ON.
         And the whole
unblocked field of their vision
hammers to get in my head.

2

Wheels of rain rock
through the streets.
They roll on the roof.
The sound of the water running
like teeth down the gutters.
Sons and their fathers.
         Daughters,
their mothers.

To be ice. To snap
brittle with cold.
To feel only this tightening
death under glass – how it fights
to get out!

           Just a moth.
Crush its soft wings
till they sift in the palm
to fine powder.
                Then small
household pets. The cat
in its elegant sleep, warming
the mohair blanket.
                  Squeeze
its fine head in your hands,
hear the bones
            crack
like fried fat.

At last your arm plunging
down through their flesh.
Slash at the children for laughing.
Rip the veins out of his neck.
Spit at them blind blind blind.

4

Oh loveless woman! Oh woman hauling huge sacks
of love you can't open! Oh woman whose lovers
bring plastic carnations! Whose husband says stop
the Chinese! Woman in smooth sheets holding

jars of dried roses! Who listens to Coltrane
in a gondola! Oh whore when the young move in!

Oh woman whose beauty was tulips, who sang
in your skin whether or not they were waiting!
Whose skin grows coarse under lotions! Whose
children are leaving and leaving! Who lies
in your own dark lacquer, dying behind your eyes!

Oh Rilke's girl at the window alone! And you
pouring tea at your table, the guests bumping
elbows and talking! And you in your milky
bath with aphorisms and bowls of daisies!
Buying tickets, fingering velvet, filling bags
in the supermarket. Alone. On the eighteenth
floor of the bank building and at sunrise
and in the dentist's chair. Alone.

5

And when the rage comes
    from a hive of hornets
walls of the house
    swell thick and hot

when the rage comes
    like the dead who aren't buried
doors won't open
    and the rooms stink

it has no way
    as water has of going
on down rivers
    to the impassive sea

when the rage comes
    she bangs her fist
hard in my eye
    to make me know

how the heart
    sticks out like a toe
through a worn sock

and how it stays there
    staring
through the live hole

It is nothing we feel
    where our shoes
    stay still
    as they are

    where we lean
over pegs
        to the bronze ball
swaying
        its highlights
over the pit
        where the earth
rotates calm
        as a saucer
and the swing
        goes wider
than any
        small swing
    of our heads.

It moves
    though the shift
    of the ball never changes
    except in the eye.

It is not to be measured
    the world creaking slowly
    the tilt of a landscape
    the falling of things.

It's the floor
        that keeps turning
        outside of the mind.

the pull of the tides
        oncoming of seasons
        your breath
        moving
        into my skin.

"AND THE EARTH WILL SLIP FROM UNDER ONE AND ONE
SHALL FALL WITH ONE'S EYES ON HEAVEN."

Pascal

There she goes, falling
to the soft light that reddens hills and walls,
    all sides that shelter.
Even the four dark sparrows on her roof's
    peak shift the sky
rosy among them, push off into it
    like larger cinders.

    She listens for the music
she has lost, rolls over warmer air,
    flapping her skin past
windows wide to heaven. Never looks down
    to see the earth turned
skyward, wrinkled, staggering with fire,
    to find familiar trees

    some branch to hide in
and the leaves still cool above the burning
    where she touched and gave.
Not there, but up, up through the glittering
    algae of the night, up
with the other believers. Never discovers
    the available rocks.

The old man sitting on the roof
is really there. In fact,
he is an uncle.
And if the wagon gets up
off the road, it's only
one leap to roll sideways
over the town.

Such leaning and loving
high in the night sky,
who will come down?
Peddlers, sweethearts,
milkmaids with faces floating
or three-breasted dancers?

Your father in his herring shop
may have seen his fish
climb ladders, but you
conform to your own miracles,
flutter your own air.

The poet finds his head turned
upside down. The weightless
angel is in the child.
The child has wings.
The fiddle is musician,
plays itself.
What is earthbound?
Which of us must fall?

To Masaccio

Seeing his *La Cacciata dal Paradiso*

You painted
them as though you too were dispossessed.
You must have seen that place, ringing with birds,
stems growing and sunlight shaking the leaves.
You had to see it once the way it was.
Until, unsure of His own faithfulness,
He began to test the only faithful.

And where it ended, you began. For them.
I watch that naked man become himself,
and Eve, all bone again, woman and pain,
move slowly, human, into their private fear.
Out of the landscape of her mouth I hear
the cry, more terrible than any, being first.
She can't forgive her breasts. He hides his eyes
as a child, blindfolded in a game, still
hides from invisible angels, flaming swords.

Here on a wall in Florence, Maso, dead
at twenty-six, you knew what they knew:
the shape of every wilderness, so many
gardens gone, the animals all named,
the gates guarded. Each of us asking
where is there left to go?

Watts

FOR SABATINO (SAM) RODIA, BUILDER OF THE TOWERS,
WHO DIED IN MARTINEZ, CALIFORNIA, JULY 16, 1965,
BEFORE THE RIOTS.

I

My friend who married the girl I
introduced him to after he felt
my breasts under the steering wheel
of his parents' borrowed DeSoto,
and swims in a big jar
in the San Fernando Valley,

my friend who plucks tonsils
with manicured tweezers, and gave me
a Barlach woodcut of two agonized
women for my last birthday,
                                        tells me
he's learning to shoot
with his children, teaching them how
with a gun, and last week
he hit the bull's eye at fifty feet
twenty times out of twenty.

The son who sings in the choir
wins prizes. The youngest, a girl,
plays the flute and the cello.
The middle one studies hard.

Why?
I ask
wanting to start over.
    Why?

    We all need a gun
    in the house. Learn
    to use one. The first time
    I fired it, they jumped.
    Now they love it. And Watts,
he says.
    Think about Watts.

2

Monday morning and the red garbage
truck shifts up the hill, jerking
like bones, like California
sliding in the sea.
                  Bent,
with the big can full to his shoulder,
cigar in his teeth, tattoo on his arm,
and two flat boxes of slimy lettuce,
chicken bones, sardine cans,
used-up carbons stuck to his hands,
he climbs the path to the street
and heaves the dreck in.
                      What
do we keep?

3

I went to Watts to see
the Towers. To see the sky

come at me
in thin frames, bleached
by the bluer glass.
                    The Towers.
Flying like ladders, testing
a coolness that we never
reach.
            As if I raised
myself into that breach, as if
I climbed on coiled springs
                              into air.
(Taylor over the keyboard
                              lifting
the sound so fast his hands
are spaces that the wind
pours through.)

                    Broken mirrors,
and my face in parts,
the shapes of corn ears,
baskets, one thin shoe.

Thirty-three years, Rodia,
card number 6719 in the International
Hod Carriers, Building and Common
Laborers' Union, his single
trowel slapping the wet cement,
bending the hoops to let
the light come in, lifting
the junk, the junk
                    to spires!

The way trees grow and slowly,
ring over ring.

                    Plates,
abalone shells, bottles,
lengths of pipe.

                    Against
his death.

4.

Guns in warm houses,
rifles. Knives.

                    Glass
in the streets and burned-out
doors.

        I'm saving
finger nails, peeled skin,
cut-off hair, lives
of insects, cancelled stamps,
semen and spit,
                    even
my shadows, reflections
in water, footprints in dust.
Dead leaves and babies,
canceled maps.
                    Mountains
of anything, falling
snow,
        my body
a tower of glass the wind
cracks through.

They are deep
And we come all this way
to look down where
the treasure is gone.

It's always the last time.
I am smoothing a thin gold
mask to your face
as weightless as faith
in my hands

We climb
and the dry grass shakes
in the wind. It is burning
the edge of the graves.

The room is already old.
Mounds of soft earth
swell slowly. You
are making me
disappear.

Stone gates,
tense lions, the white sun
stopped in my groin. I am thinking
of when to be born.

II

from Gold Country
1973

You are sitting on the edge
of our bed naked
leaning over your knees
your elbows resting
on them and your palms
cupping your face

you do not know me
speaking to your back
naked I speak to the light
along your spine
your smooth shoulders

wondering if you turn
your face perhaps
it will belong
to somebody else
perhaps the woman
lying here
will not be me

what we imagine
is
in some real place
but where

Degas said an artist
finds a hand so beautiful
he can shut himself in a room
the rest of his life
and paint fingernails

the smallest part
but every day to discover
what he knows

I could look at your back
all day like this
and memorize each muscle
how the skin
shines over them

the rest of my life
speak into your silence
if I believed
you recognized my voice
or where
it was coming from.

FROM THE APHORISMS OF ANTONIO PORCHIA,
TRANSLATED BY W.S. MERWIN

I

All that I have lost I find at every
step, and remember that I have lost it.

> Grass. It all comes separate
> in shining pieces when I
> lie down in it.

> The humming
> begins. Damp, inhabited caves
> I had forgotten, huge bones
> no longer waltzing.

> Games
> in the dark, that bearded
> saint turned serpent,
> redeemable only with kisses
> under the fern.

> I entertain
> myself, a carrion in the weeds,
> feeder and fed-upon.

> But the small girl
> rocking in my joints won't
> be absolved. She keeps
> catching moths, watching them
> smother in a jar.

A great deal that I no longer continue,
within myself, continues there on its own.

    All night long I give away your suits,
    wool at my fingers, jointed,
    having their own seams,
    putting the cat outside.

    I stay behind the window
    watching us run.

                What you send
    back to me bounces
    against a net. Trees bend
    to scratch their shadows.
    Water flows.

             And pride.
    How it sits there like dust
    on the shutters.
    Infects the air.

The chains that bind us most closely
are the ones we have broken.

When the ground crumbles
under our house and the storm
moves down the gutters and gales
loosen the roof, we let go.

The clock stops stunned where we are
locked in our arms inside the case
and toppling over.

                    And if
I reach the open
from the pendulum's box, escape
the knocking of bronze,
and in a raging wind recover
my breath,

                    why
does your face define my fingers,
why do we move against our mouths
into our mouths' dark habit, why
does the throat's soft ticking
make perilous lies?

Would there be this eternal seeking
if the found existed?

Someone comes up to you keeping
his hands closed. He goes
to everyone. "What have I got
in my hand?"

You think
that what you want most
must be hidden there. Right one
or left. You beg him
to open his fist.

And finally
he does. Look how the skin
lies curdled in his palm.

I know what I have given you. I
do not know what you have received.

I am combing my hair at the top
of the glass mountain.

A steep slope
of language
zigzags
from me to you.

You will break
your neck on it.

You know exactly
what you have said.

You do not
know what I have heard.

The Dream

AFTER DÜRER

You are dreaming yourself
into the sixteenth century
comfortably wedged between pillows
and a warm tile stove
while the devil in wings like a bat
squeezes a bellows at your ear.

You are dreaming yourself
into Venus with her hard nipples
and her hand stretched out
coaxing you to tickle her palm.

Perhaps you even see Cupid
playing on stilts
with a Fortune ball.

You feel it throb in the dream.
Laziness is the Root of all Sin.
Virtue and Vice tug at both ends.

I am as pitiless as light
waking you
in a strange bed.

Realities

FOR GEORGE OPPEN

When I've been warm
a long time, I don't think of any
fever in the absence of wind,
hum of a few bees, orange cat
dozing in the sun.

                   The idea
I have of myself is the thing
that's corrupted. To move
from that,

             turning down sheets
at night, the skin
shines on the knuckles, fingers
pull at the fabric. Arm's swing,
shift of the elbow, stretch
at the wrist. Alive. My self
and nobody's mother.

The rest is comment.

          Or
one could say: stars
grass the mountain
letting them be.

But we continue,
"Yes, I see," meaning

42

not what the eye takes in
but what we know along with it

or maybe after
when we look again.

The way I hold this prism
to the sun

                turning it sideways
to refract the light

until I see the rainbow
not the glass
the seven colors passing
through my hand.

Her face breaking all over
in little pieces standing up shouting
shit man yeah yeah shaking her hair
like feathers in the dark the man
on the screen splits into three
jerking his arms his legs his neck
three heads six hands now squeeze
the cool sound between his fingers
squeeze the snakes out of his guitar
and three round mouths moan love ya
in the mike pressing it like three
women to his lips

               and leather
rocking smooth in front out of electric
funnels beads

             they slap the seats
they bounce around me break down fences
to the launching pad

                  under their plastic
blankets in the rain slide down
the mud laughing mud in your eyes
your ears there lies the future
but you can't get hold of it sliding
and sliding in the mud

               loving
they call it loving
city bodies naked in the pond

nursing babies while the sun
beats time it's bright
and no one's fighting
in tall grass beside the field
they are taking their clothes off

slowly his pants her blouse his
socks her bra the music insists we can
hear it white flesh now the high
notes grow red grow purple
stain my whole mouth like berries
under the sky they are
berries hundreds of thousands
of berries swaying with their hair.

Shall I let my teeth sail out of my head
higher hug the drummer higher
do handstands on my seat higher shall I
tear up my passport and my credit cards
make my own music out of the dead
years amplified higher come back come
back cut my sleeves into fringes
fly

    out of it   suddenly
it's over and the last sound goes
like a stone dropped into water I can't
find it and the last endless garbage
catches fire and the last car
starts down the highway nothing is
certain only it

               happened

                    there.

No use waiting for it to stop
raining in my face like a wet towel
having to catch a plane.
to pick the apples from her tree
and bring them home.

The safest place to be
is under the branches. She
in her bed and her mouth
dry in the dry room.
Don't go out in the rain.

I stretch my arms for apples
anyway, feel how the ripe ones
slide in my hands like cups
that want to be perfect. Juices
locked up in the skin.

She used to slice them in quarters,
cut through the core,
open the inside out. Fingers
steady on the knife, expert
at stripping things.

Sometimes she split them sideways
into halves to let a star break
from the center with tight seeds,
because I wanted that,
five petals in the flesh.

Flavor of apples inhaled as flowers,
not even biting them.
Apples at lunch or after school
like soup, a fragrance rising
in the steam, eat and be well.

I bring the peeled fruit to her
where she lies, carve it
in narrow sections, celery white,
place them between her fingers,
Mother, eat. And be well.

Sit where her brown eyes
empty out the light, watching
her mind slip backwards
on the pillow, swallowing
apples, swallowing her life.

They changed her name
to Nellie. All the girls.
To be American.
And cut her hair.

She couldn't give up
what she thought she lost.
Streets like ceiling cracks
she looked up watching
where the same boy bicycled always
to the gate of her Russian house.
She saw him tremble
in the steam over her tea
after the samovar was gone.
She was Anna Karenina
married to somebody else.

    *

Oh she was beautiful. She could turn
into an egret with copper hair.
She could turn into a fig tree.
She could turn into a Siberian wolfhound.
She could turn into an opal
turning green. She could drown us
in the lake of her soft skin.

Rhythm of chopping garlic
motion as language in her wrists

warming her hands
rubbing it
over the leg of lamb.

*

Leaving the kitchen she would cry
over pictures telling us
nothing new

till the small light by her bed
kept getting lost under the blanket
where she crawled looking
for something she forgot
or money in her old house
under the hankies looking
for spare parts.

She swallowed what we brought
because we said to.

*

The rabbi knows
the 23rd psalm backwards
and he pretends he came for a wedding.

Do me a favor she still pleads
under the roses
begging for proof of faithfulness
or love. If I say yes
she might ask anything like
stay with me
or take me home.

It's my face staring
out of her picture
wrinkled and old
as a newborn infant

pushed there
ahead of myself

or memorizing lines
over and over in a soundproof room
until the smile is stuck there
and the lips stay frozen
like a hole in the ice
where a child fell in.

The Burning of the Birds

Flight songs the way they build their nests –
all were miraculous.

Montezuma's water birds had ten lakes
emptied cleaned and refilled every day.
Salt water for sea birds
seven thousand feet high
and private pools for birds
from marshes and streams.

He could watch from the palace balcony
a ring of ibises herons flamingos
feeding at his gold-sandaled feet.

Hundreds of keepers cared for them
collecting molted feathers to make
bracelets and banners feathered fans
robes trailing shadows of the gods.

Bird-gods or god-birds shapes that flew
or skimmed the lakes like tropical flowers.
Sun was the quail or was the quail the sun?
Lord of them all the war god
beak of a bird's head covered with down.

And Cortés burned them
quetzals lovely cotingas hyacinth macaws.

To see how their wings like torches
filled with flame and remember that burning

every burning when the end is ashes
and the wings tip over in the smoke

to think of their pampered wings
the well-laid fire
how their colors flaked into it
beating against that brilliance till they fried

to hear the air scream their panic
turned into outrage into words
repeated like birds or seasons
or the outrage of history repeated
which is the same as fire or burning feathers.

Plumes of the quetzal
god-filled iridescence and the human blood
shriek in the air over and over
bright birds falling scorched
in the oven of their wings
as dead as any dream of paradise.

III

from From One Life to Another
1979

She is astonished by the moon
as she crawls out of the sea
on a small island, dragging
the male crab on her tail.

He hangs there by the hooks
he's just grown out of his legs,
clutching at what she
offers him, and half her size.

She wears him as she wears
her great shell like a mask
stretched over her body
and the steaming eggs.

Air enters her gills
like moonlight
and she breathes it on this
one night out of the water

with her sisters, and their
ferocious lovers
hanging on. Already
the tide slips back,

and on the beach the crabs
are giddy, meaning to go.
They always mean to.
Four hundred million years

of habit, still they are caught
like shards left over
when the roof falls in.
They lie at sunrise

in the bright sand, holding
the dark inside them,
dreaming of floors of oceans
where they move alone.

Ossabaw Island

Bunk Beds

I

My face in the mirror and his eyes
back of my eyes and back
of us both the money carefully
counted in a purse like licorice
buttons, bottle caps,

or *groszy* in Ulanov, mud
in the streets where you can't
see it, up to your ankles
as you find your way to the river,
lose and find it again.

Poland, whatever they call it
when the borders change,
a river of mud where
nobody fishes, Poland
around you like a swamp.

His brother reads Schiller
by the small lamp
at the toll bridge, all
the unholy books you never
should open. His secret

longing to be keeper
of the bridge like Jack,
to read the books in German
stopping the wagons
to collect the tolls.

Books and money. Money and never mind
the books. You might say water
under the bridge or mud,
or how do you feed a wife
and child. Telling us money

got him to the next town,
money bought him a coat
that wasn't his brother's, money
peddling eggs from door to door
so he could buy the ticket

to America where there was more
of it in bunk beds
than anyone dreamed. Everything
smelled of varnish even
in spring. He cut the cost

and piled them one on top
of the other like blocks or bricks
or candy bars, like pieces
of dough you play with
till the stuff gets spongy,

doubles in size. You
punch it down and watch it
rise, cinnamon buns,
the Dow Jones, what do you
think? It grows on trees?

3

There in the photograph his smile
suggests what passes for happiness,
the slight blur of his arm
feeling the weight of the biggest
salmon he ever caught.

When he had trouble sleeping
he told me he thought of salmon
on his line, reeling
the big ones in, their scales
in the sun like silver coins.

I hold his hand until
the soft skin tightens with a
jerk and I let go. His head
strains upward and his lips
as if the air is somewhere

beyond his reach, as if
he sucks a pineapple soda
while the small bits of fruit
get stuck in the straw. It is his
death he sucks on and it comes

in quick gasps thicker than
syrup at the bottom of the glass.
His mouth gives up then, open
and round like a young trout, size
of a dollar with the dollar gone.

1

She said a white cloud
followed them up the hill
and hovered above the crazy androgynous
phoenix with its plump white breasts
like lids of sugar bowls.

Both of them noticed it
and told each other later.
So I didn't just make it up,
she said. It looked like the soft
underside of an egret's wing.

When they had stood a long time
over his ashes, the cloud
turned into smoke or steam
or shimmeriness, that was the word
she wanted, and was gone.

2

In Taos we eat sopapilla
with honey butter at La Cosina
and pay one dollar to see
the obscene paintings, banned in London,
by the author of *Lady Chatterley's Lover*.

They fly back into paradise
as he kept running through
the gates of the wrong gardens.

He went to Mexico and almost died.
Back to the ranch. But didn't stay.

When Frieda returned to Taos
with his ashes, she forgot them
on the train. They had to
flag the train down at the next stop
to get them back again.

3

Someone keeps looking in the window,
stealing Brett's paintings off the wall,
the drawings she made of him.
The sun's too bright. That's why
her eyes are covered with milk.

She has to be lifted, heavy
lumps of her, into the chair.
She turns up her hearing aid.
Ah Lawrence. Telling us how
she touched him to make him calm.

And she goes on about the cabin,
and the horses dragging the wood in,
Photographs of her quite
beautiful and slender next to a tree
or in a doorway, watching him.

4

A lizard runs over Frieda's tomb,
his green tail longer than the rest
of his body. There are fresh

pine boughs on the ground.
And a visitor's book

full of ecstatic letters
to the dead. Someone pasted
a poem in the little chapel
over two roses in a bottle.
So many women in love,

their souls like small eggs
spilling out of their shells.
Outside the phoenix sweats
in its white plaster,
unable to rise.

T'ai Chi

FOR JOSEPH KRISS (1919–1989)

You get out of bed each morning
and do T'ai Chi.
You feel like clouds, like steam
with its fuzzy little particles.
You scoop up space in your arms
and bend slowly letting it spill.
Circles ripple around you
where you turn on the pin
of your own center,
rain falls
in a puddle of rain.

You tell me the story of the serpent
and the crane. The crane
stabs over and over
with its beak. The snake,
as quick as anything that flies,
curves out of reach.
They each take turns
at yielding.
You want to learn
the perfect balance
of that dance.

Now the dark sockets
of your body yearn
toward perfection.
You feel each disc of your spine
lift

as you rise on the journey
that takes you out
and back again.
You walk on water, softly
the inside of your leg
comes toward you.

Carry tiger to mountain,
grasp the bird's tail.

You do T'ai Chi
without a sound. I watch
how your muscles find
your bones, your intricate
structure being held,
how it can topple
to the ground.

Like hands making shadows
on a wall, you move
your wrists.
There is an unseen ball
you take in your arms
as you step lightly
balancing air, balancing
your breath till it goes
out of you.

Leah

...BUT RACHEL WAS BEAUTIFUL....

Genesis 29:17

I do what I have to
like an obedient daughter
or a dog. Not for your fingers
in my flesh. I watch you
every day as you watch her.
Since I'm the ugly one,
the one pushed into your bed
at night when you can't
tell the difference.

I've got another
son inside me, and still
you watch her. She doesn't
sag as I do after each birth
until you fill me again.

Why can't you look at me
in daylight, or take
my hand and press it
against your mouth?
I'm not a stone, a shell
your foot rolls over
in the sand. The life
gone out of it.
Maybe I am.
Your sons have sucked me
empty and dull.

I leave your tent at dawn
and walk to the river where I
throw my clothes off,
and the water shows me
my body floating
on the surface. It shivers
when I touch the blue dome
of your unborn child.
I touch my unwanted self
where the smooth skin
stretches over my breasts,
the silver veins. I'm cold.

I enter the water
as you enter me. Quick.
Like insects doing it while
they fly. The shock of it
lifts me,
and I swim raging
against the stream.

The pipes froze
there's no more
water in the house
use the outdoors they say

I go through trees
the wet leaves thick
under my feet
small pouches of snow
strange on the California ground

finding a place to squat
ridiculous woman
my ass
          speckled
with cold

    *

But then the statue
of the girl in bronze shining
over herself her thumb
pressed in the soft flesh of her waist
the long curve of her neck
and shoulder following the smooth line

down to her elbow her left hand
turning around her calf she is all
rhythm bending to her foot feeling
the run of her blood
under her skin the glow

of her back highlight of the small
rise at the spine's base deep
shade where her buttocks begin

*

So that I hide from old friends
and the museum is full

so that I meet you
easy the fine rain
powders my skin
it will slide off like hair-thin petals
milkweed falling through air

rain
the whole sky in motion
and my face taking it
like a freshness of earth
turned over

*

I will be
weightless
in the blue waves
of your room

or in the sunlight
looking across the tense curve
of the bridge

while you in the vivid foreground
stand
as in a bas-relief

surf whitens your shoulders
and you tell me how
the breakers came at home
crashing over the beaches
and your breath knocked
out of you sometimes
riding them
with your body only

What we discover
for the first time
is the thing we've known
having this morning
in another's eyes

or how the sky
is with the bridge
against it

it sways there
slightly
fixed in its own elation

*

Oh the pure seriousness
of pleasure

hum of gas in the oven
on and off on and off
keeping the temperature even

having and giving

darkness

        and light
around your wrist
like summer
moving between my legs

and out of your eyes
that dark in the last moment
when the wave

lifts

wholly out of itself

High over the bridge
the cold air stings
our mouths our breath
comes in white circles

there is a lid of ice
where the ditch runs

you break a sheet of it
hold it a minute
brittle with sun

it shatters
when you toss it in the road

the sky lies drying
on the broken bits

why didn't I say
I broke the mirror too

or invented a puzzle
cracked in sharp little pieces

slivers keep turning up
under my feet

I can't walk around without
my shoes

*

The sun lets itself down
in pale yellow
over the Farallones
small mouth of a burned-out mountain lost
in the sea

and the city floats
out of the bay
a mirage of long marriage

we can hear only
a deep hum rising
from the bottom
in the cold
where the buildings huddle together

    *

Three sandpipers
run on the shore
their skinny feet spread out
in opposite directions

soft white bellies
one jump ahead of the tide

    *

Old intricate lives
we are so delicately stitched

peritoneum
three layers of muscle

subcutaneous tissue
skin

   each layer
sutured tightly
over the wounds

would you undo that?

   *

Perfect small cancers
growing
in perfect
         small
                 bodies
of laboratory mice

quicker than birds
when we reach out to them

their panic

even in the clean
wood shavings

   *

We fumble toward sex
like old men
who repeat the same story
forgetting
repeat it again

if you untie that balloon
it's going to go up
and you'll never get it down

＊

Listen I want to explain
there's no nightingale
in our pillows

what strains in our throats
is our own blood

excesses I'm given to
lately

it's the impurities
that color the stone
that ultimate blue-white diamond

did you hear that did you
hear even a diamond breaks
with one hard blow

you only have to find
the line of weakness

＊

We press our hearts
against the bed to keep
from hearing them

It stops in a cold room in Brooklyn
in a language I can't understand

I take off my rings
and hold my palms together
like a small boat

you lift the folded paper over them
you look down into water

there is no end to it
it falls
in my shaking hands

All day the geese fly south
in their old departures

nights when you sleep
among the dead
your hair keeps growing
out of your skin

nothing is casual
sometimes
you feel like swimming away
inside yourself
as if the time and place
already converged

if you go forward long enough
you'll come around
to the back door

the world is full of chances
to miss
even if the key fits
you mustn't go in

this is where you
                    begin

So this is the way
you leave the old country
where they're practicing awareness
in the hot tubs
at Big Sur.

So this is the way
you leave the mother
tongue that stays
in the mouth that feeds it
but keeps quiet.

You can't learn two
landscapes in one
life he said
or a language
to put them in.

Picasso couldn't
learn arithmetic
because the number 7
looked like a nose
upside down.

So this is the way
you stand on your head
in Jerusalem: the wind
is the sea at Point Lobos
beating against the rocks.

There is a tiny wind in our room
where the fan hums
it moves the hands of the clock
like the fine hairs on your back
in every direction
we are going nowhere

all day we swam in the sea
to learn how water
lifts us from our lives
waves that we kept repeating

wherever we are
there are things we can count on
when I wake before dawn
the room is already light

Looking at Henry Moore's Elephant Skull
Etchings in Jerusalem During the War

It wants to be somewhere else
remembering anything somewhere
private where it can lie down

floating in the warm belly
of the Dead Sea

so that the skull keeps
growing in the room

and the loose skin

until the whole head sees
its feet

from a great distance.

    *

Heavy as earth is heavy
under its weight

it's the same skin
wrinkled on the back of hills

grey in the early morning
on the Jericho Road.

    *

The brain scooped out of it
lets in the light
we knew at the beginning

when our eyes were dazzled

pushed
without wanting to be pushed

out of the dark.

*

The mind of the elephant
has nothing to lose

*

I was begging you
not to go
when you closed the door

and left me
watching the skull's
round openings

the eyelids gone.

*

There are caverns
under our feet
with rivers running deep in them.

They hide
in the sides of cliffs
at Rosh Hanikra
where the sea breaks in.

There is a way to enter
if you remember
where you came from

how to breathe under water
make love in a trap.

    *

Step over the small bones
lightly when you feel them
tripping your feet.

    *

Fear hangs over your shoulder
like a gun it digs in my arm

but the live head knows
that the eyes get used to darkness

fingers learn how to read
the signs they touch.

    *

Ditches where bones stand up
and shake their fists at us

sons in the shadows
and the shadows flattened
like grass rolled over

one-eyed Cyclops
slit of a concrete bunker
we prowl through
looking for flowers.

*

We are going down a long slide
into the secret chamber
we bought our tickets for the ride

the passage is narrow
and we can't find ourselves
in the trick mirrors

we lie down in the fetal position
back to back
each of us in his own eye socket

marvelous holes
the mind looked out of
filling with dust.

*

My lips on the small
rise of forehead above your eyes

mouths of the women in Ramallah
who spit when the soldiers go by

huge head of an infant
shoved out of the birth canal

faces stretched over us like tents
wet bandages over burns

and the white skull balder
than rock under the smile.

      *

If the smooth joining of the bone
makes arches from here to there

if the intricate structure yields
arms resting desert landscapes mother and child

if the thin membranes and the thick
weep in the naked bone

then the whole elephant can rise up
out of its flesh

as in the torso of Apollo

something is pulsing
in the vacant skull

making us change.

      *

I don't want to stand
on our balcony with the lights out

black buildings
street lamps
and headlights turned off

and nothing
against the sky

the stars get closer
but it's not the same
as what you plug in.

    *

There's an elephant inside me
crowding me out
he sees Jerusalem
through my eyes my skin
is stretched tight
over the elephant's skin his wrinkles
begin to break through
I taste the coarse hairs
crowding the back of my mouth
I fall down gagging over my four feet
my nose turns into a tongue with nostrils

it starts to grow.

    *

I see bodies in the morning kneel
over graves and bodies under them
the skin burned off
their bones laid out in all the cold
tunnels under the world.

there is a photograph in the next room
of a dead child
withered against its mother
between the dry beans of her breasts

there is no blood
under the shrunk skin

their skulls are already visible.

  *

The elephants come after us
in herds now
they will roll over us
like tanks
we are too sad to move

our skulls
much smaller than theirs
begin to shine.

Dinosaur Tracks in Beit Zayit

How there is anything so old
we can't imagine
anyone not there
to see them

three fingers
out of touch with each other

scars under my sole
like an old cut starting
to hurt again

when I put my foot
over his foot
I move in the same direction

    *

Everything dies in its own language
even before we find the name
and we remember only
what we can put together
what do I know about
pain in the bones of an old man
or those feet
always having to risk how far to go.

    *

Next to the broken stones
in a small clearing
the sky is pale
as if it never got over the long night

and the white dust that gathered
where they fell
comes like sleep over my eyes

if I keep walking over the earth's rim
I'll disappear.

*

In less than the time it takes
to get from one life to another
we move closer together

I want to say to you
where are the children

the wind can't get in
where our shoulders touch.

*

Someone is digging next to her front door
she is planting a rose garden
her spade hits rock
she scoops the earth away
uncovering footprints

she thinks about everything
under her going
somewhere it doesn't arrive

at night when everyone's sleeping
she hears the silence of the world.

Take Anything

I

I know a beautiful woman
with frugal eyes
who has written a book on Pain.
She tells me about the privilege
as if it were money.
The privilege of pain.
If you don't have it,
how will you know its absence?

Take anything
and imagine its absence:
the house we go back to
every night, a rock
too heavy to be moved,
fish jumping in the pond.

I put myself in the window
looking across the rock pile
to the pond. The house
is gone the rock is gone
the fish are gone. Even the pond
where we looked at ourselves
in each other.

But we are here.
I feel your breath along my tongue.
Something enters my head
like the fish splashing and the pond
breaking and mending, breaking
and mending in the sun.

At the end of summer an east wind
blows from the desert
like a visible flame, blue
under the smoky light,
sucking the moisture from the air
that shrivels around our heads.

The fresh mint growing in the pots
wilts and gets spindly.
We blame everything on the weather.
If you don't feel it, you haven't
lived here long enough, they say.

The heat drifts out the door
when the moon rises.

3

Swimming in Puget Sound at night
when we were children, our skin glowed
in the phosphorescent water.
We shook the light off as we ran
shivering to the great log fire.
The driftwood sang like jungles,
and we danced ourselves warm around it,
close as we dared, and closer
till I slipped on the wet sand.
Somebody pulled me out and rolled me
in blankets while the sparks
rose over me like stars
and the smoke whitened my white lips.

We saw the bronze head of Hadrian
covered with centuries of clay
the day they found it
in a plowed field. The curls
were tight around his neat head
catching the sun. The tip
of his perfect nose shone
through the grit.

To test a rumor, Hadrian chained
a line of slaves and threw them
into the Dead Sea, proving
a man could drown but not sink
in those oily waters.

Can you imagine the long pain
privilege for anyone drowning
in his own death, wanting to sink?

My mother taking six years to die.
The last time I saw her there were
bruises all over her shoulders
where they strapped her in the chair.

5

Now at the bottom of the world
the Dead Sea moans
and clots of tar rise to the surface
like rotting bodies. We watch them
spread into greasy stains.

This is the place, you say,
as if pointing to light
in the old paintings, how it
comes from a source itself unlit
preceding the painter.
If you don't see it,
how will you know its absence?

Take anything unburied
from the old life when they all ran
screaming up the beach. Pain
moves from the center slowly
like the sound of a plucked string
dwindling into space.

I strain to hear it
as I keep floating face up
in the salt.

The Mountain

I

In the morning I am alone in the icy room
everyone has gone to climb the mountain
the only sound is the noise in my head
machine of my anger or my fear
that won't shut off
the wind keeps cranking it.

My daughter has fled to the mountain
a piece of her dress in my hand
it is green
and I hold it next to my ear
to stop the wind.

What she took out of me
was not what I meant to give.
She hears strange voices,
I dream she's the child I grew up with
kneeling beside her hamsters
soft things she cared for
cradling them in her hands.

I want to make my words into a hamster
and nest them in her palms
to be sorry again
when she falls out of the tree
and breaks her arm.

She runs to an empty house
with her own prophets

they sit shoulder to shoulder
waiting for the sky to open
they can already see through a tiny crack
where the path begins.

2

Yesterday we saw how roots of mangroves
suck the warm sea at the desert's edge
and keep the salt
the leaves are white
and flaky as dead skin. My ankles swell.
I must be drowning in my own brine.

A Bedouin woman stands veiled
in the ruined courtyard. There's a well
a hole in the ground
where she leads the camel by a rope
I watch her fill the bucket
and the camel drinks
lifting its small shrewd head
rinsing its teeth with a swollen tongue.

The woman is covered in black
her body her head her whole face black
except for the skin around her eyes.

My daughter watches me watch her
with the same eyes.

She picks up a handful of rocks
and hits the camel
shrieking she strikes it
over and over to make it move.

I am alone in the icy room
everyone has gone to climb the mountain
the only sound is the woman
chasing the camel with the rocks.

I look out at the dry river bed.
I let her go.

Because the branches hang down with blossoms
for only a few weeks, lavender clumps
that let go quickly
and drop to the ground,

because the flowers are so delicate
even their motion through the air
bruises them,
and they lie where they fall
like tiny pouches of shriveled skin,

because our lives are sagging with marvels
ready to fail us,
clusters of faces drifting away,

what's settled for is not nearly
what we are after, claims
we keep making or are made on us.
But the recurrence of change
can still surprise us, lilac
that darts and flickers
like the iridescent head of a fly,
and the tree making us
look again.

The hills slide eastward into the desert
from the Mount of Olives,
a slow process the natives ignore.
The coffee is sweet and bitter
in the small cups.

What are you doing in Jerusalem?

A donkey staggers over the slope
of the cemetery, carrying a load of rocks.
Everything glitters.
Everything's hammered by the sun
into bright mica.

Only the dead are dull.
They have all the answers.

It's a clear day. When I turn
I can see the mountains of Moab
renewing themselves in the blue distance
on the other side.

The Dead Sea shines at the bottom of the world
like the black, original water.

Keep trying to tell them why I am here
but none of it's true:
fabric I cling to
the way a child drags her torn blanket
in the dark.

And the stray cats mew between my ankles
as if they remembered me.

We know what we want
before we know who we are.

That's why the angels
go up and down the ladder all night
with our petitions.

That's why a woman
opens her legs
with her eyes closed.

That's why I came down
out of the air, unsure
as each of us in the first
departure, everyone telling me
this is home.

Brest Litovsk

My mother remembered how she sat
in the cart beside her father
when he rode through the lands
of the absent landlord collecting the rents.

It was near Brest Litovsk,
the names kept changing and the peasants
would stare at them and pay.

Peasant to grandfather, Pole to Jew
each greasing the other,
steps that went nowhere
like the road to the border.

When the Cossacks came charging through the town
they bolted the doors and windows
and hid under the beds. They put pillows
over the children's mouths
to stop their cries.

There was no summer in this landscape,
even the language disappeared.
Fifty years later all she remembered
was her father's white shirt,
that he was always clean.

Pillows of goose down,
snow in the winter

where my mother walked
in the ditches of sorrow,
thick braids splashing between her shoulders,

or sat by the lamp they lit early
while the young man read Pushkin
leaning against her knees.

It rained in Seattle even in June.
She made fine stitches in her sheets
and waited. French knots and gossip.
The distance between them
was a hole through the center of the world
the rain kept filling. The rain
made a river in her ribs
on which her sad heart drifted.

There are words that can't travel,
threads that have lost their way home.

Honey

Fridays my father came home
for the weekend smelling of damp wool.

He knew there were things more lavish
than his Morris chair, but he sank into it
loosening his tie, and letting me
smooth the fur of his eyebrows
with my doll's comb.

He told me his mother put honey
on his tongue the first day at *heder*
to sweeten his whole life.

Peddlers dragging the dry goods
in their sacks: how much did they carry
from Ulanov over the toll bridge
to anywhere else?

Or in a suitcase. What else
could he do with his sweet talk,
8 by 10 photos of early American
pseudocolonial imitation maple beds?

Weeks when the doors kept slamming
and nothing would sell.
It rained in Eugene and Portland.
It rained in Spokane. And the sky
in Seattle would never turn off.

He said there was a restaurant
in Pocatello where the food moved

on a conveyor belt past his table
while he ate as much as he pleased.

Trickle of honey
in the one-night towns.

When he kissed my mother
her mouth was closed.

Wherever We're Not

It wasn't like paradise, the first place
where we huddled together
lighting the birthday candles,
catching the rain in the attic,
or stood on a bench
extending our wings as far
as our fingers, and fell
on the floor.

Home we keep saying, the keys in our pocket,
as if there's a refuge
nothing can change.

How the same rooms console us briefly
when we return, the bed
and the table with its lamp.
The heaven of small lit porches
when the sun goes down.

A big fly lurches from window
to window in my room, crazy
for anything out there.

Aunt Fan in a pleated skirt
won't take her medicine or eat.
She keeps her slippers on all day
over her sagging stockings,
dabbing "White Shoulders" behind her ears
as if Vronsky were coming.

She doesn't belong in Seattle,
no one is good enough, the first
one still follows her
home from school.

She wants me to know it.
She wants me to see her
loosen her raisin-colored hair.
She wants me to climb with her backwards
into deserted dachas,
to lie down on the damp boards,
plaster crumbling around her
as he unbuttons her blouse.

His face is fuzzy in the dim light
but I feel his hands.

Nights when their faces press hard
at the windows and their scalps shine
pink and almost transparent
under the thin hair, their breath
makes thumbprints on the glass.

Grandpa sucks on a cube
of sugar, sipping his tea.

They are all in the kitchen
with their new names,
stirring the rusty language,
spilling it into their saucers
to let it cool.

Steam rises like dust from their bodies.

My grandmother fell down the stairs
and broke her hip. She died
in a Catholic hospital, as far
from the Czar as she could get
without crossing another ocean,
nailed through the bone.

Her wig's on the night stand,
stiff little nest
the birds have abandoned.

Nothing I think of
will add up to theirs, will add up
to nothing at all. There is no equivalent for silence,
no silence thick as the bundles
around their ankles, no
place to return to.

My father sat on the toilet
reading; my mother kept talking
through the door.

If you think of the worst
that can happen, he said, you won't
be afraid.

A child who listens behind the door
to trouble, trouble.

Didn't they keep it
to themselves? All night
the road out of Poland
and all day the rain.

Ashamed of the language
like hand-me-down sweaters
the rich cousin gives
when you want something new.

The immigrant dustbin.
You shake out the past
as you shake out the cloth after dinner,
but your tongue is under the window
catching the crumbs.

If I go down to the docks
in Seattle where the ferries
are loading for the next trip,
or watch how the lights come on
in their pale fuzz as I'm walking
home through the rain, my mother's still
wiping the dust from the lampshades
with a damp rag, crying.

If I go down to the Judean desert
where the cliffs line up
on their knees to face the sunrise,
sages come out of their caves
like old lovers with their *gematria*
and their ancient scrolls
and their promises of redemption.

Less insistent than she is.
A dark head bobbing out of the cistern,
refusing to drown.

When I stand on this ridge,
the earth slides helpless
in two directions. There's only
Jerusalem on my left, everyone
climbing over the corpses,
on my right the frozen wilderness,
black goats looking for something green.

Stones

When you live in Jerusalem you begin
to feel the weight of stones.
You begin to know the word
was made stone, not flesh.

They dwell among us. They crawl
up the hillsides and lie down
on each other to build a wall.
They don't care about prayers,
the small slips of paper
we feed them between the cracks.

They stamp at the earth
until the air runs out
and nothing can grow.

They stare at the sun without blinking
and when they've had enough,
make holes in the sky
so the rain will run down their faces.

They sprawl all over the town
with their pitted bodies. They want
to be water, but nobody
strikes them anymore.

Sometimes at night I hear them
licking the wind to drive it crazy.
There's a huge rock lying on my chest
and I can't get up.

Déjà Vu

Whatever they wanted for their sons
will be wanted forever, success,
the right wife, they should be
good to their mothers.

One day they meet at the rock
where Isaac was cut free
at the last minute. Sarah stands
with her shoes off under the dome
showing the tourists with their Minoltas
around their necks the place
where Mohammed flew up to heaven.
Hagar is on her knees
in the women's section praying.

They bump into each other at the door,
the dark still heavy on their backs
like the future always coming after them.
Sarah wants to find out what happened
to Ishmael but is afraid to ask.
Hagar's lips make a crooked seam
over her accusations.

They know that the world is flat,
and if they move to the edge
they're sure to fall over. They know
they can only follow their own feet
the way they came.
Jet planes fly over their heads

as they walk out of each other's lives
like the last time, silent, not mentioning

the angels of god and the bright
miracles of birth and water. Not telling
that the boys are gone.

The air ticks slowly. It's August
and the heat is sick of itself
waiting all summer for rain.

Sarah is in her cool villa.
She keeps her eyes on the pot
so it won't boil over.
She brings the food to the table
where he's already seated
reading the afternoon paper
or listening to the news,
the common corruptions they don't
even speak about now.
Guess who I met she says, dipping
into the *hummus*.

Hagar shops in the market.
There's a run on chickens, the grapes
are finished and the plums are soft.
She fills her bag with warm bread
fresh from the oven thinking
there's nothing to forgive,
I got what I wanted
from the old man.
The flight in the wilderness
is a morning stroll.
She buys a kilo of ripe figs. She
climbs the dusty path home.

Forty-one contestants in the seventh annual
International Harp Contest are trying out
at the Jerusalem YMCA. The lecture
goes on in the next room.

Sheep in the City of David.

They move in their dumb heaviness
past the houses where the boy leads them
into the field. Past the dim little crèche
and the candles eating their hearts out
in soft puddles of wax.

Like the wick that runs out of itself.
The plucking of strings.

Now the king has a headache.
We lean back together,
waiting for the music to begin.

Abishag

...AND LET HER LIE IN THY BOSOM THAT THE LORD MY
KING MAY GET HEAT.

I Kings 1:2

That's what they ordered for the old man
to dangle around his neck
send currents of fever
through his phlegmatic nerves, something
like rabbit fur, silky,
or maybe a goat-hair blanket
to tickle his chin.

He can do nothing else
but wear her, pluck at her body
like a lost bird pecking in winter.
He spreads her out
like a road map, trying
to find his way from one point
to another, unable.

She thinks if she pinches
his hand it will turn to powder.
She feels his thin claws, his wings
spread over her like arms, not bones
but feathers ready to fall.
She suffers the jerk

of his feeble legs. Take it easy.
she tells him, cruelly

submissive in her bright flesh.
He's cold from the fear
of death, the sorrow
of failure, night after night
he shivers with her breasts
against him like an accusation,
her mouth slightly open,
her hair spilling everywhere.

At ten the siren warns us to stop
what we are doing and remember the dead
whom nobody warns.

They are not listening.
They could be nodding there forever
in Lvov, Vilna, Bialystok, plucking
their kosher chickens, dealing
in second-hand pants or salt herring.
It is the summer of 1939.

All those couples strolling as the reel turns
in the gardens of the Duke's palace,
blinking in the strong light.

All those children stretched out at rest time
on the lawn of the Workers' Summer Camp
with their sticky fingers.

A man sleeps on a bench in the park
as if he owned it, as if
he might wake up out of the movie
opulent in California.

There are lace curtains in the windows
of Dr. Zamenhof's house
through which the sun cuts holes
in the universal language.

A woman arranges the blanket
over her baby in the carriage.
How careful she is
to get the edges straight.

Crumbs

Strange – what they tell us
now, the ones who have died
for a minute and come back,
hooked to machines and bottles.
They recall how the world
dropped off the sill into
daylight, how they hovered
a little above their last breath
while their eyes were fixed
on a dazzling point in the distance,
bright gleam on the water
like a prize held out to an infant
learning to walk.

One light is as good as another,
desire transforms us
to the end. Still I'd like to believe
they saw what my grandfather
prayed for.

When I was a child my mother
took me to his synagogue
on the most holy day. We climbed
to the women's gallery, so hot
in Indian summer, bodies
buttoned up and weak from fasting,
somebody always fainted.
Grandma held a vial of ammonia
in her blue-veined hand

and poured some into her hankie,
sniffing it up her nose.
Fasting and fainting, I knew then
that God was too much for me.

Sometimes at dusk I watch
the devoted at the Western Wall
who jerk their shoulders, sway
and bow, ecstatic and blind.

And there's an old man on Jaffa Road
who sits on the sidewalk selling
prayers. All day he squats
in his rags against the storefront,
holding out little blessings
on pieces of paper.

I've run from a flock of elders
through my whole life, fidgety
sparrows dropping crumbs
from their small beaks
to show the lost children
the way through the forest.

By what fervor, nailed
on our doorposts, worn as a sign
between the eyes, can we
manage our lives?
By what diligence of faith
give them up?

Fawn

The fawn we rescued on the road
to Nes Harim where dogs
had cornered it, its mother gone,
refuses the bottled milk,

refuses the logic of our hands.
The smallest offer makes it
tremble on skinny legs
that barely stand.

It is trying to keep
its bones together, the ponds
of its eyes won't focus.
They reflect nothing.
It is too soon.

Stroke the head, the silky
place between the ears.

We can only invent
what we think it needs.

And red poppies.
And after the flower-spattered hills
the Dead Sea. Sunlight
peeling off the old skin.

Not wondering how it happened.
So that the surface floats
on its warm back, smiling.

So that the body loosens itself
to kindness. The one thing
we're ready for.

Walking across the park in April
when the blossoms were out
you told me you felt so young again you wanted
to take my hand and swing it
running away at fifty falling in love
you said yes falling because the plunge
begins in heaven with the angels
falling they hold us under their wings
to break the fall.

I tell you what I remember
as we climb the uneven terrace,
vineyards they never dreamed of
washed away. How I left them
and left their expectations
and left again.

The first time you brought me
to these eroded hillsides
and we drove past the rush
of silver in the pines,
I wouldn't believe
it was sewage from the town.

Sometimes when you're working
in your room, I stand in the doorway
just to know you are there.

The Dream of Completion

When asked for a sample of his work
Giotto took a red pencil,
drew a perfect circle
free hand
and sent it to the Pope.

What does it mean
to be that sure of anything?
The dream of completion.
We cross the field
with the small stones biting our sandals,
picking up shards.

Sometimes you finish
what I think I've said.

We take the clay fragments,
skin-colored, bits of them worn
or crumbling between our fingers,
and piece them together.
Something is always missing.

Leaves are the color of burned-out
trucks on the road to Jerusalem. Obsolete
armor. Grapes in the market
already smell of wine,
and the flies tap sugar
from their overstuffed skins.

We think we can smell the rain too,
smashing its tiny mirrors in the north
as if what we waited for
might come.

Chosen for what? The live carp
flap in their vats. They think
they should be flying.
I take one home in a plastic bag.

We get down on the floor at first
because the kittens are there
and it's easy to play with them.
Fierce little faces. Sakhar
shows me her favorite,
lifting its chin.

Where can it lead? From her home
in this Arab city, her taut friends
over the teacups. The color
of license plates tells us
who we are.

I might have stayed
on my own side where it's common
to say the wrong things
and be forgiven.

It's not just a matter of truth
or occupation.
We each have our fables,
the sweet cakes
stick to our fingers as we speak.

The kittens roll over
and the mother finds them,
nursing one hunger at a time.

The widows forget nothing.
When they open a window, the wind
is the breath of their anger
knocking things over.

The bare stones blind them.
If they close their eyes
a dark space enters. They keep it
under their eyelids when they sleep.

In the morning the space
surprises them in their beds.
It stands in the mirror
while they brush their hair.

At home after work
they prepare the meal. They serve
the cold soup at the table.
The space is there.

Even when they take off
their black scarves. Even
when the children grow up.
They are not consoled.

The widows forget nothing.
It's no good telling them
that their loss
is everyone's loss.

Over my head
the Bengal ficus
dangles its roots like seaweed
out of the sea, licking
the ashes from the air.

Sure of which way is down
but unable to get there,
one tree makes a hundred
out of the steaming soil it comes from,
replanting itself.

Not here.
The roots are shaggy
with trying in this land.
No earth, no water,
what are they doing
in the light?

Trees find their shapes again,
as the world blanches. It must be morning.

At the window I can make out the dim outlines
of the domes the towers lit by the dawn.

On the sill the dove sleeps
over her two damp birds.
She built a nest in the pot of geraniums
and yesterday they hatched,
little homemade bombs.
They are not Jews or Arabs.

I go to the center of the world
near the edge of Jerusalem
where the grapes are all picked
and the men are climbing
into the olive trees.

I watch how they beat the branches
and the dark fruit drops to the ground.
The families move in and out
of the dust to gather them.

October again.
The rains are coming, the steep cold
and the festering idleness.

The women are sorting the bitter crop.
In the empty fields small
clusters of lavender petals
explode from the soil
without any warning, not even
a stem or a single leaf.
A kind of privilege. As if
they earned the right
through the exacting summer.

Look! They say for a moment.

V

from Rivers of Salt
1993

After the fervor
of fists on the breast and fasting,
after the last plea slips through the heavenly gates
as they close and we've run out of things
to atone for, I want to start over.
The way my grandmother purified her heart
in the women's section.
But the rains are late, we're not forgiven,
and autumn won't come.
A few blurry showers in the north,
not in Jerusalem. No loosening.
No green rinsing of the trees.

We can't do anything
but wait. Fear sticks to our minds
like the black lice of newsprint.

The dead are so light, they don't wait,
don't have to consider what might happen.
The wind simply lifts them over.
Michael was edging off all summer,
week by week he grew lighter
until he left hardly anything behind.
A man grows small in the distance
as he unwillingly walks away, walks backwards
so we can see the little twist
of his smile. His face already taut as a mask
from which his breath trickled out.

Last week clouds came, a dark insensible mass
above the hills, but nothing fell. We wait

in front of an empty screen
when the movie is over and the next one hasn't begun.
Too dull or dazed to get out of our seats.
Someone is sweeping the refuse
in the aisles. Someone is torching
a car in the next block. Someone
is shooting into a gang of boys.
Someone is slashing open a woman with a knife.

Students at the vocational high school are printing
a book of poems. In celebration, they tell me.
Will you give us a poem?

We walked to his grave on the mountain
in a dry wind, our backs to the sun,
crossing an endless grid, hundreds
of empty plots evenly bordered with cement,
mingy homes for the homeless
waiting to be assigned.
"He will make peace...for us..."
When they finished the *Kaddish*
the men took turns and shoveled the soil back.

Autumn won't come, but the days are shorter
leaving us suddenly.
The heat never closes its eyes.
Staying up with the moths
and the souls of the lost ones
we're not really stranded. We just have to
lie here in the dark, soothed after love,
getting used to how it is.

There are black rubber masks in our closet.
When you tighten the buckles

and smooth the rubber snugly over your face

and attach the filter according to the printed instructions,
you can breathe fresh air
for about six hours. That's what they tell us.

Celebration. A poem. One of the birds
that woke me up today sang three notes
over and over. We stood on the balcony
watching them fly from the roof
and the eaves next door
in and out of the pines with their flawless wings.
It has to be one of the common birds,
you said, a bulbul or greenfinch.
It can't be a jay. They mostly screech.
Maybe a blackbird. Quick, on the branch.
Flicking its yellow beak,
it took off. One sunbird
dangled below us giving off sparks.
There were high-pitched calls
and a steady twitter. Most likely
it was a crested lark, you said,
but I can't tell you how any of them sing.

November, 1990

Not for their ice-pick eyes,
their weeping willow hair,
and their clenched fists beating at heaven.
Not for their warnings, predictions
of doom. But what they promised.
I don't care if their beards
are mildewed, and the ladders
are broken. Let them go on
picking the wormy fruit. Let the one
with the yoke around his neck
climb out of the cistern.
Let them come down from the heights
in their radiant despair
like the Sankei Juko dancers descending
on ropes, down from these hills
to the earth of their first existence.
Let them follow the track
we've cut on the sides of mountains
into the desert, and stumble again
through the great rift, littered
with bones and the walls of cities.
Let them sift through the ashes
with their burned hands. Let them
tell us what will come after.

Tight little curls fleecing the hills
like the new growth on shorn lambs.
On the way down
it is green for awhile from the last rain,
the skin of the earth still tender.

I wish you would tell me we are not
driving through a deep moat, dark
palisades of stone, unscalable walls
above us and the crows circling
in their black coats.

The sky is slick as a sheet of plastic
over the Dead Sea. And we settle
our bodies on it, face up,
fixed in the unappeasable salt.
No matter how hard we pull each other down,
we discover we cannot sink.

It goes on burning in his brain
after the last war: standing
on guard in the desert at night
he'd watch a great blast of fire
he knew would destroy him. At sunset
the cliffs of Sinai open their veins.
The Red Sea closes over the chariots.
We think it will never end
all summer, his chain-smoking, jumpy
fingers during our visits in the ward.
There are redwoods in California
that feed for months on the heat
of their own destruction. You can see
where fires have guzzled their way
to the core, until the tree,
what's left of it, stands
gaping around its absence.

Once I lived in a house
that trapped the sun.
The walls were smooth adobe.
I could hear the clay breathe
through little straw beaks.
At night my body stayed warm
with what it remembered.

*

What lets us be who we most are?
Suppose we only had to know
the climate, what grows where,
how rich or shallow the soil is.
A kind of field guide
for dislocated souls:
how to be rooted, how to be
born in an ancient cycle
from seed to seed,
dust of our old selves settling
over a new season.

*

Sometimes I hear the siren
for the first time and the air
doesn't shiver, only my bare legs
running across the field, the dry
summer grass and the dusty thistles.
That was three wars ago.
I drove down to Jericho

to find you during the cease-fire.
I baked your favorite cake,
the lemon sponge, and we sat for awhile
together next to your gun.

*

You have to get used to fear,
not fear exactly, but a long unease.
To walk it off in the streets
and supermarket. You have to
get used to God,
wrote Elsa Lasker-Schüler,
as if he were food
one cultivates a taste for.

*

There are days when I feel like
an infant's rattle. A little
shake. A little smile,
Not yet, we keep saying
as if time were benevolent.
Last night I dreamed
we were speeding in a car,
too far from home
to know where home was.
I had tied the frayed ends
of my seat belt in a double knot.
Wasn't that strange? and the sky
fading, white-hot at noon,
powdery as plaster. It wasn't the dream
that upset me, but your face
when I told you, troubled and distant,
not asking what happened next.

I THE STATUS QUO

The sand is still hot in September
everyone drives to the beach and we float
in our light bodies watching the red ball
roll to the bottom of the sky and the sea
darken and the waves lift us
willingly toward the shore as if
nothing has happened we can go back
to the same life never mind that it's gone
like a road in the desert after a flash flood
like the houses we blew up yesterday

In Benares I saw corpses
carried high in saffron robes
to the sacred fires. We carry
these photographs as offerings
to the night. Not like the blind
who walk forever with their arms out.
Not like the holy men smeared with ashes
on the way to the temples.
But like a family, too long on the road,
who by their lassitude
have let this happen.

We walk silent through the streets,
some holding torches, others
dark blow-ups of all the slain children.
Small mouths of disbelief,
how stunned they are
in the young faces.

Second Anniversary
December, 1989

This morning after her second cup of coffee, finishing
the front page, she decides the future no longer
matters. What a relief. And the past too. Always
stepping into the next ruin, balancing on the next
ledge, making it crumble again. Ancient eroded
vineyards in the Judean hills. She can forget
what happened, all that pile-up of memory and guilt
like accidents on the bridge when the cars smash
into each other behind the first collision. We don't
have to hold our necks, she thinks with a sweet release,
or assess the damage or take notes from the other driver.
It doesn't matter it doesn't. She keeps the news
to herself like a secret drinker, not able to give it up.
The boy with his leg blown off. The dutiful children.
What she is in her own eyes, the bulk of her fear.
Yesterday she had to decide between chocolate-orange
and mocha-pecan. The best ice cream in Tel Aviv
they told her. Decide. Decide. As if her life
were the life she'd chosen. As if anyone's life

For you also, your desk at the window
in the next room, the tip of the cypress
turns like a green wrist

lifting the long tree after it.
Something flutters the ivy on the walls
across the street, blue

widens between the two pines.
Sudden. Out of the ache and heaviness.
The simmering heat.

Once in Sarnath we saw those unwinged
beings over the Buddha's head
fly upward, weightless.

We thought that the world could change
like the wind's direction. The clean sweep
of falling in love.

Blessed be whatever sprinkles
a little water on the dust
to make it settle.

That spring he was fourteen,
sun on the walls, stale air
sweet in Bergen-Belsen for the first time,
he told me he thought of the nurse
who held him when he was small.
He found a corner
where they did not catch him:
rush of the brilliance and the heat
and no one there. He opened his clothes,
hunched over his wasted body,
and made it spill.

*

The poem wants to look forward, not
back, but out there as far as it can see
are ruins: body of Abel body of god body
of smoke. And no recognizable
child to mourn.

So it begins with longing.
Or with fear, that old dog
stinking beside it, scabby and blind.

And all the time the future
is pushing up uncalled for
under the cold ground, or gliding down
like the first snow, wet syllables
that melt and soak up the darkness.

The poem wants to get out
of where it is. But is instructed
to remember. In shameless daylight.
By the rivers of salt.

After the Leningrad trials, after solitary confinement
most of eleven years in a Siberian Gulag, he told us
this story. One slice of sour black bread a day.
He trimmed off the crust and saved it for the last
since it was the best part. Crunchy, even a little sweet.
Then he crumbled the slice into many pieces. And ate
them, one crumb at a time. So they lasted all day. Not
the cup of hot water. First he warmed his hands around it.
Then he rubbed the cup up and down his chest to warm his
body. And drank it fast. Why, we asked him, why not
like the bread? Sometimes, he said, there was more hot
water in the jug the guard wheeled around to the prisoners.
Sometimes a guard would ladle a second cup. It helped
to believe in such kindness.

Snow in Jerusalem

After it stops the air is still
whirling around our house and the pine trees
shake out their iced wings the way
dogs shed the sea from their bodies
after a swim, a white crust slides
like shingles down the backs of the branches,
soft clumps loosen themselves from
sills and ledges, fall past our window
with the swoosh of small birds
or of moths at night that beat themselves
senseless against the lamp until
we switch it off and reach for each other,
warm and slightly unraveled under
the worn nap, under the flannel
of the snow sky, under the overhanging
sorrow of the city listening to the
plop, plop, it's all coming clean now,
starting to thaw a little from the inside.

You were the reason for staying.
It's always the children who leave,
not the mother. It was the end
of winter, isn't that always
the best time. Freesias suddenly
out of the mud, little milk teeth,
plum trees unbuttoned and the sky
on the Bayshore freeway to the airport
lined with blue tile.

Do you feel abandoned,
now you are women?

     ✳

From the ridge of our mountain
we can see the Judean wilderness
slide to the bottom of the world.

Sometimes the parched air ripples
with dust as if everyone's beating
carpets and the shudder of wind
is like nervous laughter out of the caves.

It's all getting smaller and farther.
The earth wears a thin green fuzz
where the sheep graze
stubby in the distance as if
they were cut out and pasted there.

     ✳

I've learned what he knows,
how to tell sonic booms from the others.
To mean what we say.

First thing in the morning
in the Valley of the Cross
when the night is still drying
on the leaves and the red poppies
stand up straight
as if pulled by strings,

a man balances on his head
in the wet grass, we're behind
two Ethiopian joggers
and a woman walking her boxer.

The rest of it empty
like the future no one plans for.

*

There's an overwrought smell of jasmine,
tiny wax flowers, wiry stems
around the railing of our balcony.
Too tame to fly, the vines
catch on and keep climbing.

Scent of my old life, where the light
falls back of my shoulders
into your day.

*

If not for the three of you, if not
for the two of us,
if not for my cousin's strawberry jam
at breakfast and a woodpecker
attacking our jacaranda
outside the kitchen window, drilling
so loud we don't hear
the seven o'clock news, if not
for persimmons and the first
green oranges we wait for
and the small hard peaches
that arrive in the market in April,
if not for the ripening
when we expect it, bulbs
of new garlic spread out to dry
just when the old garlic's rotting,
if not for Mary's latest recipes,
meat loaf with carrots and cumin
and fennel soup, and Mussa's
bottles of green-gold oil
from his olive trees in Beit Safafa,
and the crested larks, little tan females
singing their hearts out on both sides
of the green line, if not for
the bulbul's five purple eggs,
and all the glad birds on Yom Kippur
praising the parked cars
in the empty streets and the prayers
of the ones who keep praying,
if not for the archaeologist unlocking
the safe in the museum to show us
the yellowed bone, the rusty nail
still hammered through the heel,
if not for the gilded dome and the silver dome

balloons and bells
and the muezzin calling, peace
marches around the Old City wall and me
on the ramparts following my body,
if not for the two of us, waves
of white surf breaking
over the hawthorn's arthritic limbs,
if not for what flickers as joy
in the middle of grieving,
what could I say when you ask me
whether I'm happy.

*

One day I'll look up at the hills
and they won't be there. Lately
I think about my death.
It keeps me connected to the world.

I wonder if you'll come
to put little stones on me
the way Jews do to keep the unliving
where they belong.

*

I wish I could learn how
to strike matches in the wind
so they won't go out in my cupped hand.
I wish I could peel an orange
in one long ribbon that doesn't break.
I wish you were with me
in this hard land waiting for the first rain
after a long dry season

when the sky tilts and spills over
making a fresh start,
stirring the dust into muddy trickles,
clearing everything but not
washing it away.

A Japanese Fan

When I hold a chicken over the gas
to singe the blunt ends of feathers
sticking from legs and wings, the random
hairs, the loose flap dangling
over the broken neck, fat
crackles and the bumps in the skin
burn black. I pluck the singed hairs
one by one. It takes me an hour
to clean two chickens.

This morning at the bus stop on Jaffa Road
a woman was fanning herself with a paper fan.
A cherry tree and a tiny snow-covered
Mt. Fuji were painted on it.
The sun was so hot we could barely
breathe. I watched her climb slowly
up the mountain. The air got lighter.
When she wriggled her toes in her sandals,
she could feel the snow.
She wiped some of it on her cheek.

I need a Japanese fan in my kitchen.
I need a little wind to get me
from place to place.
When I tell you about the snow
my words are small origami birds
with the meanings inside.
I want you to unfold them
and look at them under the light.

The wings of this chicken
have sharp little elbows.
I have to unfold them
and flatten them over the flame.
I think of my father with his words blocked,
regarding his hands. How he was trying
to lift them, the weight
of his waxy fingers, trying
to remember what to do.
When I held his dead hand in my hand
he seemed to be holding me.

The blue flame hisses when the fat melts
and jumps into orange. One tip
of a red-hot finger over Mt. Fuji.

Milk

I

You pump it from the six goats
morning and evening
and renew your own. The baby
is harnessed to your back,
her dark head wobbling. Your life
and its order that isn't mine.

I've come as close to you
as I can. Over the sudsy milk
I watch your hands,
the little tough spots
at the tips of your fingers.
We tell it again:

how grandma stopped eating
and spit out her mush,
how the rice fields were burning,
how you stayed in your room
with the candles and incense
and played your guitar.

Once in our terrible anger
you struck at me wildly
and I couldn't see. Light
was a bolt from the laser
riveting my eye. Black flakes
floated between us for a long time.

The buckets are full. I lift
your daughter from her warm pouch
into your arms
as if I were lifting you
out of my empty body.
We're not who we are

to our mothers. Even now
in this sweet flesh
isn't there something starting
to withdraw? The child
is reminded of herself.
She wakes to cry.

2

One goat has an udder the size
of a cow's. The weight of that
huge sack slung beneath her
seems to be more than she can bear.
She struggles to stay on her feet,
and you tell me she's overbred.
Some misplaced passion for cheese
or being the best.

I warm the goat milk on your stove
and think of how scared you were
to go to school for the first time,
how you wept in my arms
because you didn't know how to read.
You thought you must know already
what you would have to learn.
The way we cry till we're red at birth
not knowing how to live.

So we perfect ourselves, wanting
to come out grander than we are,
two women trying once more
like Piranesi after fifteen years
etching his prisons again
to get them right. The great beams
are stronger than ever,
shadows are denser than before,
the space in the front left corner
that seemed to be empty
is filled with chains.

Only to see more clearly
what is there.
We stoke the Rayburn with new wood
and carry the pots of milk
out to the shed.
There is a smell of goat cheese ripening.

Men came to the door
when I was a child
and we gave them leftovers
on the back porch. Dolorous
lessons in poverty and caution.
The forms of hunger.
Deadweight of a body passed out
on the sidewalk. Nights
when my father didn't come home.
My mother brought them hot coffee,
but never asked them in.

     *

What sins did she ever, working
the heels of her hands
through the silence of flour.
Unto the next generation:
her melancholy kitchen,
the smell of turnips, lamb shanks
boiling on the stove. Peel
the potatoes for tomorrow's stew.
Roll out the dough and the flour
rises like her soft sighs
into my rocking palms.

     *

Because of the broken neck
of her first love
who fell off a horse in Poland,

and because of her marriage
to barley soup and the Depression,
and because of my stillborn sister,
and because of her amputated breasts,
and because she sang
"I'm Forever Blowing Bubbles"
until she was diapered and tied
in a wheelchair,

        *

before I could enter
the bone-china tea cups
of her memory and the Bug River
of her lost future, before
I could be her daughter,
she turned me into her mother.
Taught me the names of love
in her language: grief
and sorrow, sorrow and grief.
Translating with her shoulders
the forms of hunger.

        *

In Kiefer's painting
*Every Human Being Stands Beneath
His Own Dome of Heaven*,
rows of unplanted furrows fall off
the soft edge of the horizon
blank as the end of the world.
A tiny survivor sealed
in a glass bubble raises one arm
with no one to wave to.

A tent of pure oxygen seems
to be keeping her alive.

*

Applesauce, everything mashed
and pureed, I fed her slack body
one spoon at a time.
And then she was gone,
a house boarded up behind us.
Men sitting on the steps
in their worn clothes, eating
our last night's dinner, cold
meatloaf on white bread.
The door was open
but the screen was latched.

Lake

She is more lost to me than ever
where I stand on her birthday in the June light
next to a lake she never heard of.
The trees at the edge are dissolving
under themselves. She's not in my dreams,
she has returned to her first language,
drifting over the mountains
while my father rows the small boat.
His sleeves are rolled up
and he's milder than I remember,
though his suspenders are cutting his shoulders
and the oars blister his soft palms.
The mountains are upside down. They've left me
on the shore. I watch
how she leans back
trailing one hand in the water,
her pinned hair starting to fall down
and her eyes crinkled. I forget everything
I had to tell her. If only she'd wave
before we are gone. If only I knew
what she's saying about the future
that makes her happy.

My aunts who sit side by side
in their wheelchairs at the Seattle Home
for the Aged never wanted to be aged
in Seattle. Never wanted to be always
together, last of the sisters
and nobody left to blame.

They behave like ex-lovers, bitter
but civil when they meet in a room
full of old friends who know better.
They are not certain who we are
or why they have to go
with us to America.

Marion is strapped to her chair
and plucks at the binding around her waist.
Fan begs her to stop. Little bird bones,
they are so brittle, shrunk back almost
to what they were in the beginning.
The trunks are already in the cart.

We are trying to make them smile.
We put small squares of chocolate
between their fingers and swallow hard.
They drink the sweet milk of reproach
and the sour milk of gratitude.
It runs down their chins.

Their eyes are wide open, looking
at someone behind the mirror.

He clicks his heels. He is Polish,
with a riding crop. He's at the station
where they left him in 1912,
waiting to kiss their hands.

At the airport waiting for our plane,
we sat next to a Chinese man.
He took off his shoe and sock
and massaged his foot,
working his thumb and fingers
over the sole and delicate arch
of the instep. Then he held
his whole foot between his palms
and forgave it, rocking it
gently back and forth.
His hands seemed to know
what his foot wanted.

*

This woman pulls a thorn
from her heel and this woman
wrings water from her shampooed hair
and this woman paints her eyelids
in front of a mirror and this one
fastens bells around her ankle
and this one slips off
her transparent chemise
and this one smiles
at her dexterous lover
guiding him in.
An inexhaustible cheerfulness.

*

And sweetly convivial,
so many figures
touching and stroking
the length of their bodies,
stone warming into flesh. They repeat
and repeat each other, pleasure
runs through his fingers
to her breast and back again,
a circular comfort, the curl
at the ends of their mouths
like the tenderness after.
Even their toes curl.

                *

Touts, cripples, blind
children who pluck at our sleeves,
all the dark versions of desire
are locked out behind the fence.
Twice a day we walk to the temples
while they run after us,
past a small lake, more like a pool
of muddy water, three battered rowboats
tied up in the reeds. And a large
sign printed in English: *FLOAT*
                on the beauty of twilight
                and twinkling of stars.

                *

If we imagine hunger sometimes
it's not in our guts.
It's art we've come for,
art and the witty gods in the temples

promising bliss. We study
their postures of unresisting
grace. Your hand
slides over my shoulder.
In the half-light,
as in anything half seen,
the body remembers
what it wants to.

That's me up there on the elephant
smiling
with my mouth closed,
clutching the bar
that has just been fastened
across the box I'm caged in.

The ground seems farther
than it should be. The beggars
can't reach us.

The elephant lifts one wrinkled leg
and puts it down
and I think I'll tip over.
When there's no danger I invent it
the way I invent India.

The path is steep
all the way to the palace.
I let myself be happy a little,
squinting into the sun,
even hanging on tight. As if
I am still on my father's back,
hugging his neck,
his slippery shoulders
as he rides me to bed.

The palace is crumbling,
incandescent and pink
as the fevers of childhood,

green parrots flapping through the trees, glittery dust
on the broken tiles.

I want to be dazzled. I want
to be lifted into the room
where mirrors tremble on every surface
when a match is struck,
to look at myself on the ceiling
tinseled with light, my body
rippling in the crazed glass.

It's the same body. The same awful bulk
I sit on in the grainy air.
I just have to hold on steady
while the long sinews of the mind weave
leisurely like a trunk
that scoops up everything.

In the dark there's no other side.
Only the river where every morning
the faithful prepare for death.
Small wicks flicker in the leaves
they carry and scatter a little radiance
on their faces, their thin shawls.

Cripples are wheeled into place
on wooden platforms, and women
squat in a line on the stairs
with tin bowls. The eyes of their babies
are dull already and soft
as water in a cupped hand.
Softer than ashes.
Vague as my mother's
when they finally closed.

What is it keeps us
nurturing the first loss
with our regrets and unspeakable pity,
wanting to step over the edge
if we can come back
forgiven? What is it
in the sickrooms?

The ones who enter the river
lift the dark to their mouths.
When they loosen their saris
their arms shine. All
the wet skin of the grieved world
bobbing and rising.

How simple
the frail light is on the white shirt
of the boy I follow, led
from one boat to another
until the last one
where he unties the rope
and shoves off. And how calm
when the river takes it
and sets it down on its gray back
letting it ride there, a light
so still it scarcely seems to be
breathing. Like the light
as the fever came down
when I wrapped her all night
in wet towels, soaking and wringing
until the breath was there
in her mouth again.
It's the past I look into,
but the past keeps growing.

The boy pulls hard
on the long oars, and our boat
nudges up to the ghat
where the dead are burning.
They are shoveling the ashes
from the last one into the water.

We row with smoke in our throats
through the smoke of morning.
It's already the next life.
The sun's on the rim of the old world
like the tip of an orange thumb.
We turn toward the shore.

The widows are wrapping their heads
in white, unwrapping
their floating shoulders.
Men stand in the river slapping
laundry on the black stones.

I hear the thwack.
And the chants of praise
getting louder. And the click
of rice striking tin
in the hands of beggars, the little
pale grains collecting.

Happy Endings

I want to write stories with happy endings.
I want to write about the good life.
Even if it's somebody else's. Pliny
had a good life here in his villa.
Better than any life in Rome.
Terraces and porticos, a small hippodrome
for riding, hot and cold baths, gravel paths
between boxwood all the way down
to Bellagio. And best of all,
one room remote and quiet
where he lay in the dark each morning
composing his thoughts.

There's a spider next to Pliny's
left knee, composing his web.
Pliny's nose is broken.
He sits in his carved robes
holding a book in his hand with one finger
missing, watching the lake.
He can barely see the view
from his little stone eyes,
for the scrub and the honeysuckle have grown wild
on the cliff before him.

The spider is doing what he knows best.
He spins from the knee to the hand of the statue
as if he were swinging on a kite string
across the whole sky. The late summer air
is thick with insects. It's a good life.
Even if it's somebody else's.

He is sulking again because whatever she does
it's the wrong thing or she's talking to somebody else
and he can't stand it. But he won't tell her about it
oh no he walks away from the museum shop and she can't
find him and even up in the galleries it starts, she
wants to tell him about the Botticelli in room number nine
and he is already ahead in number eleven. And out
in the street the others are drinking capuccino at a table
on the sidewalk and they have their arms around each other
lightly and she has to ask if they've seen him and there
he is dragging his feet in the distance, studying the windows,
spending the rest of the day attached to somebody else.
And she runs after him and asks why did you leave me,
and he says he wanted to look at Bergamo or Inverness or
Jaipur and she was too busy buying postcards, and that
isn't it at all, that's never it. And what can she do
but eat lamb's testicles or crawl on her belly
through the long night or fall in the lake
with her clothes on or throw herself from the parapet.
Until he is sorry and she is sorry and they are both
sorry until the next time which is in Santorini.

I saw the hand of Rasputin
cast in bronze and used as an oversized
paperweight on someone's desk.
The authentic hand. Smooth as Italian leather.
It was molded from plaster before he was killed.
Bought at an auction in Europe.
She was a collector.
She knew the value of everything.

I wouldn't like Rasputin's hand
on my desk, even though it wore the skin
over its fine bones like a soft glove
and healed the tsarevitch.
I wouldn't like her samurai sword.
I'm glad I don't know what I'm worth.

There are days when the whole world
feels like somebody else's collection.
Even your hands. We walk
in another country and the mist
slowly rises above the lake
like all the heaviness we left,
dissolving.
Only it's not our heaviness.

     *

Sometimes, waking, I forget
where I am. The things around me
go on with their old existence
like props in a play, as if the curtain

has just risen on a room in an Italian villa.
It's not my play.

In the old life there was a photo
of Valentino on my desk.
Agnes Ayers was swooning in his arms,
the Sheik in a rapture of lips
without any words.

Benevolent uncles spoke in a language
I didn't know, their fleshy hands,
their anxious eyes smiling
as they patted me gently on the head.
Like watching a silent movie,
when they opened their mouths
like fish under water
I turned off the sound.

All that sweet absence.

                *

Once I learned the thirteen principles
of Rabbi Salanter, but I remember
only seven: truth, diligence, honor,
repose, cleanliness, frugality,
and silence. If I collected words
they would have to belong,
like moss or fleas. Things you say
that I can believe in.

Honor reminds me too much of the samurai.
I like repose. It belongs to this landscape
where even the lizards rest

when we stand still
and look at the wall together.

Naming the things of this world
you begin to own them.
Cyclamen. Mustard.
I can't manage so many flowers.
But I already know the word for lake in Italian.

*

Gulls wheel over Lago di Como
at sundown on their way south
trying to catch the last warm currents.
Their wings are white, then silver, and then smoke
when the light abandons them
and dusk settles in their feathers.

If you don't collect things,
it's easier to move. Easier to stand
on this cliff for another minute
and watch the leaves fall, one by one,
yellow, into the lake.
They belong to the air
for the time they are drifting.
It's a long way down.

VI

New Poems
1993–1996 *

Past the fierce Guardians
with their wooden scowls, past
the Great Southern Gate,
behind the bronze Buddha there's a test
for getting to Paradise.
Not sure if they're losers or winners
skinny children line up
and squirm on their bellies
through the hole at the base of a pillar.
One of them is stuck in the middle,
her shoulders won't budge.
Friends push from behind
where her feet thrash, others tug
at her arms until she emerges
red-faced and crying.

Not ready for Paradise, not even
tested, not wanting to lose
the heat of my body, I jog
until my breath slams at my ribs.
Leaves are flying all over the gardens,
tiny fans of the gingkos
spread themselves open and flutter
for the last time, yellow on yellow,
lit up, as if they have to be
luminous at the end.

At the women's college they're modeling
old kimonos to American rap.
The loose sleeves billow to the beat
of the music. I learn to suck noodles

through my closed lips, and they smile
with approval cheerfully coaxing
their grandmother to eat. Their teacher
whose name means Cedar Mountain
was a child in Nagasaki before the bomb.
"Even a lion does not eat a lion,"
he says so softly I can hardly hear
the swell of his old grief under the small
syllables and the immeasurable emptiness.
He sighs like the steppes of Asia.
"We don't say *life-and-death*
in our language," he tells me standing
on his kitchen balcony. Sheaves of rice
are hung out to dry. He shows me
the cut stalks. "We say *death-and-life*."

Pressed against the dark rail of the war
refusing to be reminded or to forget,
I look at the buds still wrapped
on the ripening kernels. I want
to be in there, unhatched and unpolished.

There are people who sit in the malls
all day in their incompleteness
gripping the handles of desire.
Something is riding on their hunched backs,
clawing their shoulders.   When they shoot
the balls madly into their slots,
neon lit marbles, little joy rides to nowhere,
they are shaking it off.

That's my face wrinkled in the pond
among the hundred year old carp.
They drift fat and golden

through the lotus. Sometimes
I wake up lying on an X-ray table
inhaling deeply, letting it out.
Strapped between my skin and the surface
of things, gold-leaf and lacquer
and the lumpish flesh, I'm waiting
for the bad news.

       If I am happy
in the carefully raked gardens, the studied
random, balance of crane and turtle
and fifteen positioned rocks,
or in our bare room where we've fallen
between the futons, light seeping
through the screen, holding   '
and being held, and if I'm glad
when water flows down the face of the granite
into its bamboo channel
the way it was meant to, is it because
I don't trust the unexpected
I used to want more of? Am I resigned
to safety? Brimming unseen in the green scrub,
the bamboo sōzu empties with a sharp crack
frightening the deer.

"Every rock has a being of its own."
The priest says he worked as a bank clerk
until he was fifty. Not wanting
his emptiness but mine, I try
to be still again the way I learned it
in the sixties. I try not to try.
To hear the leaves. This one,
for instance. The wind nudged it

from the maple as I raised my head
and already it's a lost thought,
all the colors are sailing past me.
Not the rock. How stony it is!
And weathered, like the old poems.
Tilted a little to one side
but not unbalanced.

Masako says her mother took the train
to Nara with her haiku club
to watch the full moon on the rippled sand.
What does an old woman do
with the moon in her hair all night?
What does she hear in the bright dark
when she listens to the sound
of no water under the sand?

IN THE SILENCE

ALL EXTREMES ARE ALIKE

Roberto Juarroz

When light burns from the sea
to the mountain and the jewel
in the Buddha's white granite forehead
catches fire, the sun
plows everything silver.

He's looking at nothing,
his eyes are closed

the way we distance ourselves
to see more clearly.

Stone hushed against stone,
he's done with the welling up
and the ebbing

as in the Pietà, the forbearance
even of the toes
worn down and kissed into brightness.

*

If you follow the Kyŏngju road
to the bottom of the hill
where the kings are buried
you come to a huge black tulip
turned over. The bell

wouldn't ring when they cast it
so they melted it down
and threw a child in the molten bronze.

The dragon was appeased.

How big a fire does it take
for a small soul?
Or for a small girl's body
to burn away from its cry
until only the cry lasts
out of the hollow where her ribs were
calling her mother

if we believe such stories.
That was twelve hundred years ago.
Nobody strikes it now.

*

History is a reversible rug we turn over
when the colors fade.
It lies with its face to the floor
so that we let it happen to others
or in art.

What can I do
with the dailiness of shock,
mute as the etching of a woman
holding her dead child,

its almost fluorescent head fallen back
as if the neck were broken,
bones of her hand as in an x-ray
mapping her pain.

Light blooms from the body
of a child, its weightless presence,
and a woman who knows about loss
far into the future.

Her lap supporting the infant
is a Buddha's lap.

*

I keep trying to put them
together

   his weightless shoulders
and the silenced bell

color of morning on the stone
like light returning
to the skin of my body
when I wake

or the rim of the glass
beside my bed.
Even to emptiness

    or grief
sliding down his right arm
where the hand rests easy across the leg
down the other
finger by finger
over his silky foot.

AFTER THE PAINTINGS BY RUTH LEVIN

I   SKY

Of course it is infinite
though the earth overwhelms us.
All we can see
is what we look up at
from where we are.
It makes a smooth edge
on the jagged world
stripped to its one
essential. Blue.
No moon or sun
to measure time by
so there is only the absence
of time and our need
to fill it. Gold spills
out of the tombs
and the tombs are empty.
Sand in a wilderness
of sand. The sky
granting nothing.
The persistence of
space like the smile
on a granite face.

Palm trees are planted
against the light.
Stiff with age,
they can't bend their knees.

Tall women walk by the river.
They have lost their feet,
their heads are flattened
by the weight of the sun,
bundles of thornbush they carry.

If you pass between the long
trunks of their bodies
you enter the village.
The roofs are low,
walls the color of moon
when the moon whitens
floating above the fierce lameness
of the women.

Already there's more behind them
than ahead. They stare
over the mild river
where there is no shore.

And if they wore woven air,
the ancient Egyptians, linen
garments fine as webs
over their naked bodies,
it must have been steam
from the baths or a curtain of gauze
pulled down when the light becomes
dust, or even the dust itself
on the city's eyelids.

It drifts from the domes,
unsettled after the slow
fall. No wonder we're lost.
We stir the dust as if
it were something necromantic,
neglected omens, puffs
from the Book of the Dead.

The sun stayed out of the woods
when I left the sidewalk
to grieve under the fir trees,
ferns like small rafts bobbing
in the half-light, me
floating there forsaken
on my black barge.
By the waters of Lake Washington
I sat down and wept.

Rosalie Gross got the boy
I wanted. I knew hardly anything
of pain except what she taught me.
She had a brother who was killed
in Spain. Once on the floor
of his sad room,
hunched over his books,
she talked about free love
and we swore on *Das Kapital*
that we were Reds.

                                Her hair
was the color of strong tea
and she would twist it high
on her head, not like the buns
of our mothers. We slid down
on our backs and she played me
the record for the first time,
rolled herself over, twisting
her hair till I couldn't
stand it, letting it spill

on our small breasts, the music
throbbing to its crazed fall.

Why, after so many years,
as if by that lake
when the slow dusk flattens the water
and you hear more than you can see,
why do I think about her?
Breathing on mirrors
when it's cold. Little smudge
of confusion. The wetness. The need
to be touched. Nothing more
happens for the first time.
Ravel is soppy. The trees
cut down and the paths all gone
from where they should be.

The knife was much sharper than I thought,
and severed the head. I was relieved
it stayed on her neck, although
she was bleeding across the throat
and down the shoulders from under
the bun. The whole body
stood where it was, accusing.

Sometimes in dreams she comes back
shaking her finger, whatever
I didn't. As if bewildered
by my anger, comes back
out of the twilight as the trees
darken there on our porch,
her eyes from a Russian novel.

She caresses the scar on her throat
like a string of worry beads,
calling, *you'll catch your death*,
as if it were butterflies
or fish, *this time you'll be sorry*,
all the years of my childhood calling,
still calling me home.

Nobody wants it to rain at a wedding.
Already the trees were losing their edges
to the dark behind them. Your friends
raised the *huppa* as if they were pushing
the clouds back, lifting a portable
velvet hope.

                  I wanted to lift you
again on one of the animals you chose,
swans hollowed out in the center
where we both sat, the ostrich you rode
by yourself, hanging on to its neck.
Each time you went around I'd wave.
Practicing, though I didn't know it,
for your sweet rides later, nights
I stayed up waiting like my mother
waiting to save me from the world.

Little fish on my belly. That's where
they laid you when they cut us loose.
I was afraid of your squashed face
until I saw how baffled you were,
your foggy eyes, your small mouth
begging. Sometimes I'd see in your eyes
me looking into my mother's,
sucking her angst, or grandma, tiny
and whiskered, hiding her shorn hair
under the wig like her true life
scissored in Poland.

Someone was always
sorry. We go on being the daughters,
feeling their lonely breath on our faces
after the breasts dry or after we marry
the wrong ones. Walking backwards
into our lives.

The gray sky
was coming at us like a mudslide,
you in your clean space saying
what we all say.

"The West is Suffering from Compassion Fatigue"

Mornings they rake the paths at the villa,
trim the boxwood, clear the dead pansies.

The mountains are blue all day, a cool
unflappable hush over the lake.

Before lunch we take turns with
the Herald Tribune. And over the pasta

we talk about change. Evenings we gather
in the grand salon sipping Campari

or the clear licorice of sambuca,
coffee beans floating on top.

How courteous we are. Musical voices
and phrase-book Italian and optional

lectures. Afghanistan or fish.
Slides of the swamp eel in India

slithering. Ancient air-breathing mutants
that drown in water. I think of them

gasping in the mud when the rivers dried,
glassy fish eyes exploding out of

their sockets. The ones who made it, lungs
unfolding, spongy, one lobe at a time.

Some days I stroll in circles
in a thin rain, connecting dots

in a child's puzzle, tiny blisters
of light on the wet topiary,

unnatural forms that crouch there
blinking. Some days I write poems

in the classic arbors, eased by the symmetry
of terraced gardens, the slow diligence

of natural selection. Click of the shears
as they whittle the hedges into peacocks.

Silly to think about it, traveling
like this, riding a little cage
up to my room. Reverent beside
the old cathedrals and tombs.
Who'd visit my grave? The recent
past has tissue-thin pages
I can't turn over and the print
is too small. I admire ruins
when they're not reconstructed.
And wormy armoires. A cousin

in Seattle never forgets
my birthdays that end in zero.
Gianna tells me that in Genoa
they stack the dead in a skyscraper.
They've run out of space. It seems
like a fine idea to be up there
already close to where you are going,
to wake in the brilliant core
of yourself without a body, a spine
of unalterable light.

Or perhaps right here in Pescallo
where the cemetery is smaller
than a baseball field and so many
neighbors with bunches of flowers
wave to each other on a sunny afternoon
it seems like a garden party.
There are faces on every headstone,
even the babies. How would you know

when to take the last photograph?
What sort of neckline?

Lilies and roses in the mossy urns
are freshly cut. The carnations
are paper. I rub the petals
between my fingers just to be sure.
I'd want to have real ones.
I'd want them to stand around
for awhile and wipe the dust
off my picture when they come
to pull the weeds and stir
the soil around the pansies.

There's a stainless steel door at one end
through which they've taken you, and a sign:
No Entry. I'm waiting opposite
a white rabbit with droopy brown ears
who sits in a wicker basket suspended
from a balloon. The basket is attached
to the balloon by shiny pink ribbons.
What are they dripping in your veins?
I can only see the bottom
of the balloon which is also pink
with wallpaper rosebuds painted on it.
The rest is all sky and very blue.
Very bright where the surgeon reaches
into your body. The rabbit seems puzzled
but calm, a little phlegmatic.
One fuzzy paw dangles outside
the basket as if testing the water.
His eyes are oily black olives
staring at me. This was the only
empty seat when they wheeled you away
and for five hours I have been watching
a rabbit hanging out of a basket
between pink ribbons hunched in the sky
on the wall with the wrong ears
and one irretrievable paw.

If only she could make herself
shuffle the papers on her desk
sort out what to deal with
what to dump and what to fill out
who to thank and when to pay. If only
she could arrange them neatly
the way he arranges his pills each morning.
If only she had a system of priorities –
most, more, least
terribly, very, oh well –
especially since mail had been accumulating
for weeks, months, even before it happened,
even a year. If only he went out sometimes.
If only he weren't hurting all day,
all night from the gash
in the middle of his shaved chest
and the split of his rib cage,
from the two slits up the sides
of his hairless legs. His patched body.
His pain. If only she could complain.
If only he'd answer the phone. If only
he wouldn't say why didn't you make soup.
If only he ate yogurt. If only
she could lie down alone
and sleep for ten hours. If only
she could find her glasses. If only
she could find his glasses.
If only she could write a poem.
If only they could stop watching
the news. If only they could stop looking

at the cut-up faces. If only twenty-two people
weren't blown up in the bus yesterday.
If only they could turn it off.
If only they could stop talking
about security.

We don't think we're waiting for the end,
but the end is waiting.

The mind cultivates its flaws
like an oyster.

You and I are not like the effortless ones
who are there already.
Not anything like them.

When the circuit breaks
we grope for the matches and candles.

After each night we wake
without detachment,
still needing each other.

It is the month before the leaves
fall, everything hanging on
for dear life. When I stop
on the path where lizards run
in and out of the borders, one
lizard stops with me. It chased
its shadow up the steep side
of the hill. Now it stands still
and together we study a marigold
next to the ivy. We both breathe
as softly as we can to keep it
from moving, to keep this minute
from slipping into the next.

ABOUT THE AUTHOR

SHIRLEY KAUFMAN is the author of six other books of poetry and several volumes of translations from Hebrew. A collection of her *Selected Poems*, translated into Hebrew by Aharon Shabtai and Dan Pagis, was published in Israel in 1995. Among her recent honors is the Shelley Memorial Award of the Poetry Society of America. Growing up in Seattle and living in San Francisco for many years, she has made her home in Jerusalem since 1973.

BOOK DESIGN by John D. Berry. Composition by John D. Berry & Jennifer Van West. The type is ITC Galliard, designed by Matthew Carter in 1978. Galliard is based on the 16th-century French humanist typefaces of Robert Granjon, although it is not a direct revival, and this version was digitized by Matthew Carter in 1992 for Carter & Cone Type Inc. *Printed by McNaughton & Gunn.*